BRANCH LINES AROUND HAY-ON-WYE

Vic Mitchell and Keith Smith

Cover pictures:

Front - No. 46510 stands at Three Cocks Junction with a train from Hereford on 1st October 1962, only weeks before the end of all passenger services here. (G.Adams/M.J.Stretton coll.)

Back - The Bulmer Railway Centre at Hereford was home to the 6000 Locomotive Association. Its 0-4-0 ST ***Pectin*** *was recorded at Vernons Halt in 1992. (6000 Locomotive Association)*

Published January 2007

ISBN 1 904474 92 6
978 1 904474 92 0

Design Deborah Esher
Typesetting Barbara Mitchell

Published by
Middleton Press
Easebourne Lane
Midhurst
West Sussex
GU29 9AZ
Tel: 01730 813169
Fax: 01730 812601
Email: info@middletonpress.co.uk
www.middletonpress.co.uk

Printed & bound by Biddles Ltd, Kings Lynn

CONTENTS

INDEX

ACKNOWLEDGEMENTS

We are very grateful for the assistance received from many of those mentioned in the credits also to P.G.Barnes, W.R.Burton, A.R.Carder, L.Crosier, G.Croughton, F.Hornby, F.Jeanes, N.Langridge, B.Lewis, C.G.Maggs, D.T.Rowe, Mr D. and Dr S.Salter, R.E.Toop, Dr R.W.Willé, and in particular, our always supportive wives, Barbara Mitchell and Janet Smith.

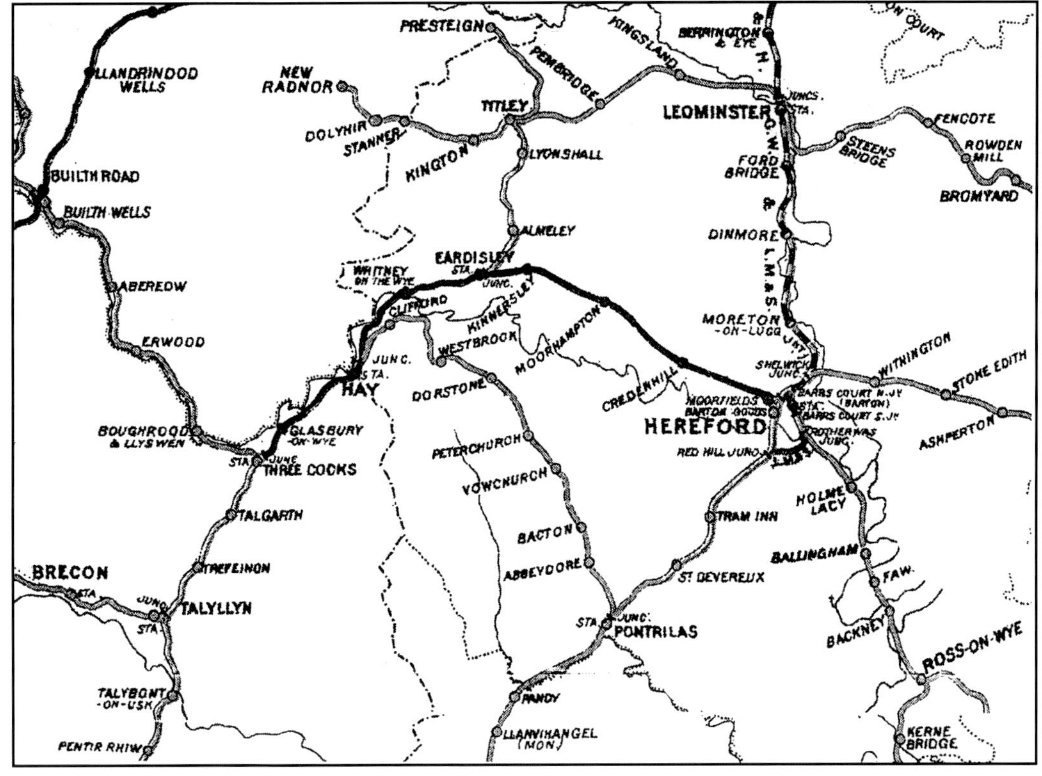

I. Railway Clearing House Map for 1947.

GEOGRAPHICAL SETTING

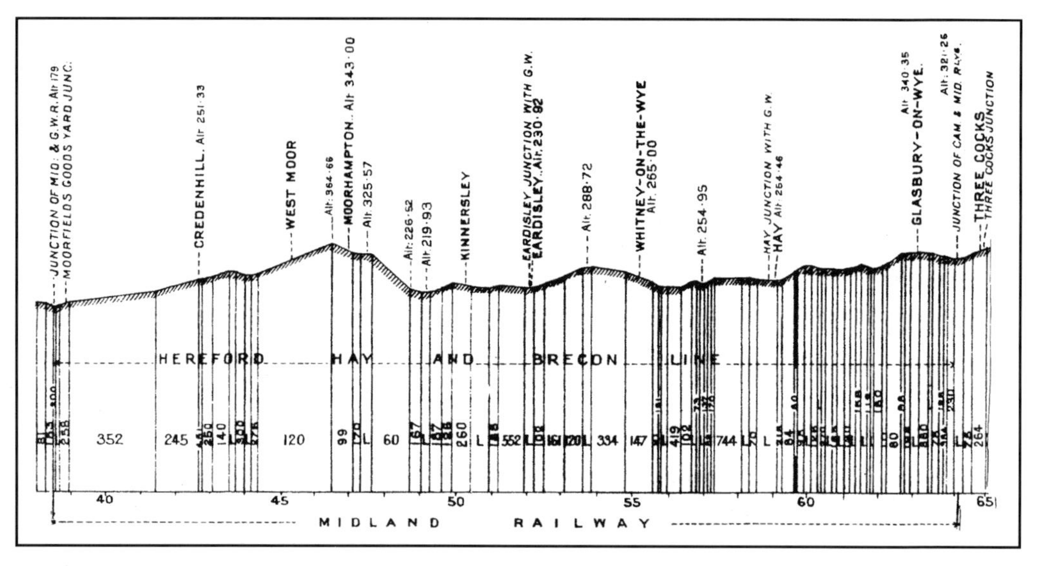

The gradient profile shows the Midland Railway's section of the route and altitude in feet.

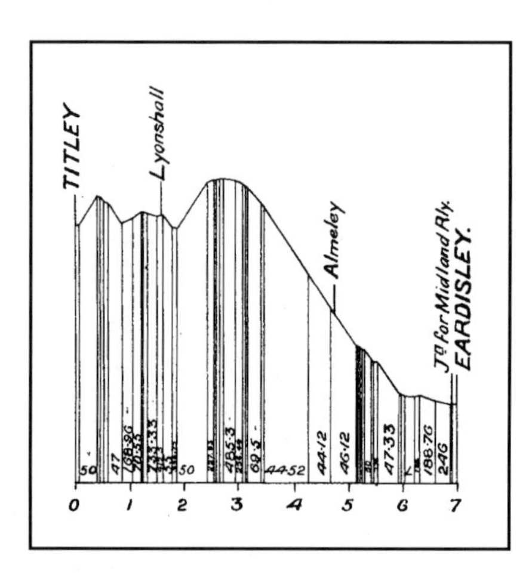

The Hereford-Three Cocks Junction line ran along the narrowing valley of the east flowing River Wye, initially the line being up to two miles north of the river, but later closer to it.

The Golden Valley line was near to the south flowing River Dore for its entire length. Its headwaters are close to the River Wye at Westbrook.

The Titley Junction to Eardisley route climbed over a ridge from the valley of the River Arrow. All the lines generally traversed Old Red Sandstone.

The maps herein are mainly to the scale of 6ins to 1 mile to show the rural environs of most stations. The enlargements are at 25ins to 1 mile. The route was predominantly in Herefordshire, the final six miles being in Breconshire.

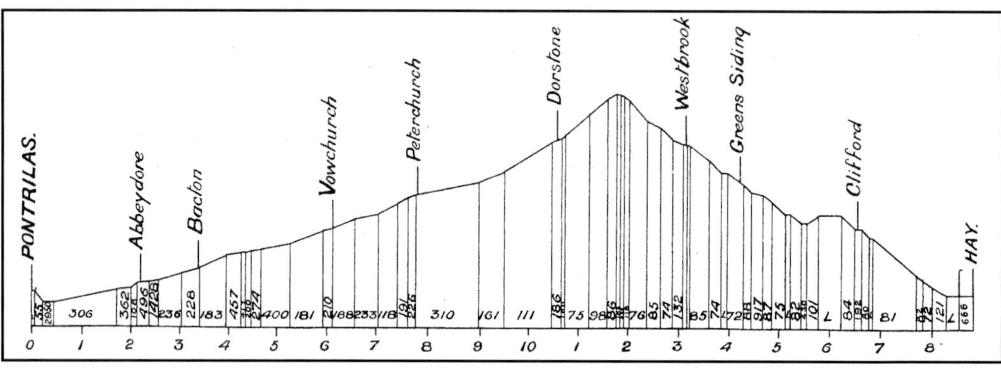

HISTORICAL BACKGROUND

Hereford's initial service was from the north when the route opened from Shrewsbury in 1853. It became a joint line under the control of the Great Western Railway and the London & North Western Railway. The route south to Newport also opened in 1853, but they had separate termini in Hereford. The complex story of creating one station is outlined in the captions. This line became part of the GWR in 1863 and this company also took control of the 1855 route to Gloucester in 1862. It carried passengers until 1964, the other two lines being still in use.

The Hay Railway Company was incorporated under an Act of 25th May 1811 and its 3ft 6ins gauge track opened on 7th May 1816 to Hay from the Brecknock & Abergavenny Canal at Brecon. On 1st December 1818 it reached Eardisley, where it connected with the Kington Railway, which served quarries in that area.

The Hereford, Hay & Brecon Railway Act was passed on 8th August 1859, but the advent of the Brecon & Merthyr Railway and the Mid-Wales Railway made a change of plan necessary. The former reached Brecon in 1863 and the latter joined it at Talyllyn Junction in 1864, running over much of the route of the Hay Railway. The HHBR thus ran only to Three Cocks Junction.

The Hereford to Moorhampton section was opened for freight on 24th October 1862 and passengers were carried following extension to Eardisley on 30th June 1863. Trains ran to Hay from 11th July 1864 and through to Brecon from 19th September of that year.

Initially the service was provided by Thomas Savin, who had constructed much of the route, but from 26th August 1865 until 5th February 1866, the GWR provided the trains, according to most accounts. From that time until 30th September 1868, it was the turn of the B&MR. The Midland Railway took over thereafter and through running to Swansea began in 1877. (It continued until 1931.) The MR took a lease in 1874 and acquired the route between Hereford and Three Cocks Junction in 1886.

The MR became a constituent of the London Midland & Scottish Railway in 1923, which mostly became the London Midland Region of British Railways with the advent of nationalisation in 1948. The route was transferred to the Western Region on 2nd April 1950, closure to passengers following on 31st December 1962, the year in which Brecon lost all such services. Freight (notably chemicals to Dowlais) continued over the line until 4th May 1964. It was truncated to Eardisley until 28th September 1964.

Titley Junction Branch

The Kington & Eardisley Railway linked the MR with the 1857 Leominster-Kington line. The branch opened on 3rd August 1874 and was operated by the GWR, which purchased it on 1st July 1897.

The former was closed for the period 1st January 1917 to 11th December 1922, as the track materials were required for military use in World War I. The final closure came on 1st July 1940. The Leominster-Kington-New Radnor branch closed in 1964.

Golden Valley Line

The Golden Valley Railway Act was passed on 13th July 1876 and the line opened north to Dorstone on 1st September 1881. It was completed to Hay on 27th May 1889, the delay being due to financial problems and bad track. (Passenger service was suspended from 2nd July to 19th August 1885.) The difficulties continued and service was suspended north of Dorstone on 23rd August 1897. Total failure came on 20th April 1898 and all traffic ceased. The GWR acquired the business, scrapped all the GVR stock and made the track safe. It operated trains over the entire line from 1st May 1901.

Following an uneventful period of decline, the passenger service was withdrawn on 15th December 1941, at a time when the southern part of the route was busy with substantial traffic for a new ordnance depot built as World War II developed. The last freight train between Dorstone and Hay ran on 31st December 1949. The progressive cut-backs of goods services are noted in the captions, the last section closing in 1969.

PASSENGER SERVICES

Hereford to Three Cocks Junction

The first part to open had three trains on weekdays and upon completion the figure was six. By 1869, the figure was four and continued the same until around 1940 when it fell to three trains on weekdays. The year before closure in 1961 the figure had risen to five trains every weekday, however even by then there was no mention of a service on Sundays.

Titley Junction Branch

In the early years the branch offered four weekday trains, which were reduced to three a day before its short period of closure from 1917. Upon reopening in 1922 the service remained at three trains every weekday, a steady figure until final closure in 1940. Again there was no evidence of a service on Sundays.

Golden Valley Line

The initial service comprised three mixed trains, plus an early morning train on Tuesday, Wednesday and Saturday, but the first and last were soon deleted. However, they all appeared in the first through timetable, plus five others and a short trip north to Dorstone in the morning.

The GWR provided a three-train service from 1901, plus a short working on Wednesday. The service was later cut back to two and eventually one. There was no evidence of Sunday operation.

June 1869

HEREFORD, HAY, and BRECON.—Mid Wales.

Miles.	Fares 1 cl. s. d.	2 cl. s. d.	3 cl. s. d.	Paddington Sta.	mrn	mrn	mrn	aft
				LONDON 8 dep	....	6 0	10 0	2 20
				Hereford b..dep	9 40	1220	3 20	8 0
4½	1 2	0 9	0 4	Credenhill	9 50	a	3 30	8 12
8½	2 0	1 6	0 8½	Moorhampton	10 0	1240	3 40	8 22
11½	2 8	1 10	0 11½	Kinnersley	10 8	....	3 50	8 32
13½	3 0	2 2	1 1½	Eardisley	1013	1253	3 55	8 40
16¾	3 8	2 7	1 4½	Whitney	1023	1 3	4 5	8 50
20½	4 6	3 2	1 8½	Hay	1033	1 13	4 15	9 3
24½	5 4	3 9	2 0½	Glasbury	1043	1 23	4 25	9 15
26	5 8	4 0	2 2	Three Cocks Junc	1050	1 28	4 30	9 20
28½	6 3	4 5	2 4½	Talgarth	11 0	1 35	4 40	9 30
31½	....	....	....	Trefeinon	....	1 41	....	....
33½	7 4	5 2	2 9½	Talyllyn Junc.	1120	1 50	5 0	9 45
37½	8 0	5 8	3 1½	Brecon 30 arr	1130	2 5	5 10	10 0

a Stops on giving notice to the Guard. b Moorfields Station.

Mls.	Fares 1 cl. s. d.	2 cl. s. d.	3 cl. s. d.	From Neath, p. 30.	mrn	mrn	aft	aft
–				Brecon dep	7 5	1010	1 5	5 40
4				Talyllyn Junc.	7 15	1020	1 20	5 50
6¾				Trefeinon	....	1024	....	....
9	1 6	1 0	0 9	Talgarth	7 30	1038	1 35	6 5
11½	2 0	1 6	0 11½	Three Cocks Junc	7 35	1050	1 45	6 15
12½	2 8	1 11	1 0½	Glasbury	7 40	1055	1 55	6 20
17	3 6	2 6	1 5	Hay	7 55	11 5	2 7	6 30
20¾	4 4	3 0	1 8½	Whitney	8 7	1115	2 17	6 39
24	5 0	3 6	2 0	Eardisley	8 16	1124	2 28	6 45
25½	5 4	3 8	2 1½	Kinnersley	8 24	1129	2 35	6 50
29	6 0	4 2	2 5	Moorhampton	8 35	1139	2 47	7 2
33½	6 10	4 10	2 9	Credenhill [27, 21]	8 45	1149	2 57	7 12
37½	8 0	5 8	3 1½	Hereford 126, arr	9 0	12 0	3 10	7 25
—	....	....	....	LONDON 11 arr	3 10	5 45	1035	4 35

All 1, 2, 3 class. Extra.—Hereford (Barton Station) to Brecon, on Wednesdays, at 4½ aft. No Sunday Trains.

June 1897

PONTRILAS, DORSTONE, and HAY.—Golden Valley.

Sec., David S. Derry.] All 1 & 3 class. [Man., F. W. Green.

Fares 1 cl.	3 cl.	From London, p. 50.	mrn	Weds. only. mrn	Thurs. and Sats. aft	aft	
		Pontrilas dep	7 15	8 50	1 5	4 40	....
0 5	0 2½	Abbeydore	7 22	8 57	1 12	4 48	....
0 11	0 6	Vowchurch	7 32	9 7	1 24	5 0	....
1 3	0 7½	Peterchurch	7 37	9 12	1 30	5 6	....
1 8	0 10½	Dorstone	7 47	9 22	1 42	5 18	....
2 8	1 1	Westbrook	....	9 33	1 52	5 28	....
2 7	1 4½	Clifford	....	9 44	2 2	5 38	....
3 0	1 7	Hay 423 arr.	....	9 50	2 10	5 45	....

Fares 1 cl.	3 cl.	Down.	mrn	Weds. only. mrn	Thurs. and Sats. aft	aft	
		Hay dep.	....	1030	3 0	6 0	....
0 5	0 2½	Clifford	....	1039	3 9	6 8	....
0 8	0 5½	Westbrook	....	1048	3 18	6 18	....
1 4	0 8½	Dorstone	7 55	1058	3 28	6 28	....
1 6	0 11	Peterchurch	8 5	11 8	3 40	6 38	....
2 0	1 1	Vowchurch	8 10	1113	3 45	6 43	....
2 9	1 5	Abbeydore	8 21	1123	3 57	6 55	....
3 0	1 7	Pontrilas 50 to 53 ar	8 28	1130	4 5	7 1	....

June 1920

PONTRILAS, DORSTONE, and HAY.—Great Western.

Miles.	Down.	Week Days only. mrn (Wednesdays only.)	mrn		aft		aft
	Pontrilas dep.	7 5	8 45	....	1 40	....	5 15
2¼	Abbeydore	7 12	8 51	....	1 46	....	5 22
3¾	Bacton	7 16	8 55	....	1 51	....	5 26
6¼	Vowchurch	7 25	9 5	....	2 0	....	5 35
7¾	Peterchurch	7 30	9 10	....	2 6	....	5 40
10¼	Dorstone	7 38	9 23	....	2 20	....	5 48
13¼	Westbrook	....	9 33	....	2 30	....	....
14¼	Greens Siding	....	9 36	....	2 33	....	....
16¼	Clifford	....	9 43	....	2 40	....	....
18¾	Hay 497 arr.	....	9 50	....	2 53	....	....

Miles.	Up.	Week Days only. mrn (Wednesdays only.)	mrn		aft		aft	
	Hay dep.	....	1025	....	3 20	....	....	....
2¼	Clifford	....	1032	....	3 25	....	....	....
4¼	Greens Siding	....	1039	....	3 30	....	....	....
5¼	Westbrook	....	1043	....	3 37	....	....	....
8½	Dorstone	7 50	1055	....	3 45	....	6 0	....
11	Peterchurch	8 0	1110	....	4 0	....	6 10	....
12½	Vowchurch	8 5	1125	....	4 10	....	6 15	....
15½	Bacton	8 13	1130	....	4 20	....	6 23	....
16¾	Abbeydore	8 19	1135	....	4 30	....	6 29	....
18¾	Pontrilas 84, 86 arr.	8 25	1150	....	4 40	....	6 35	....

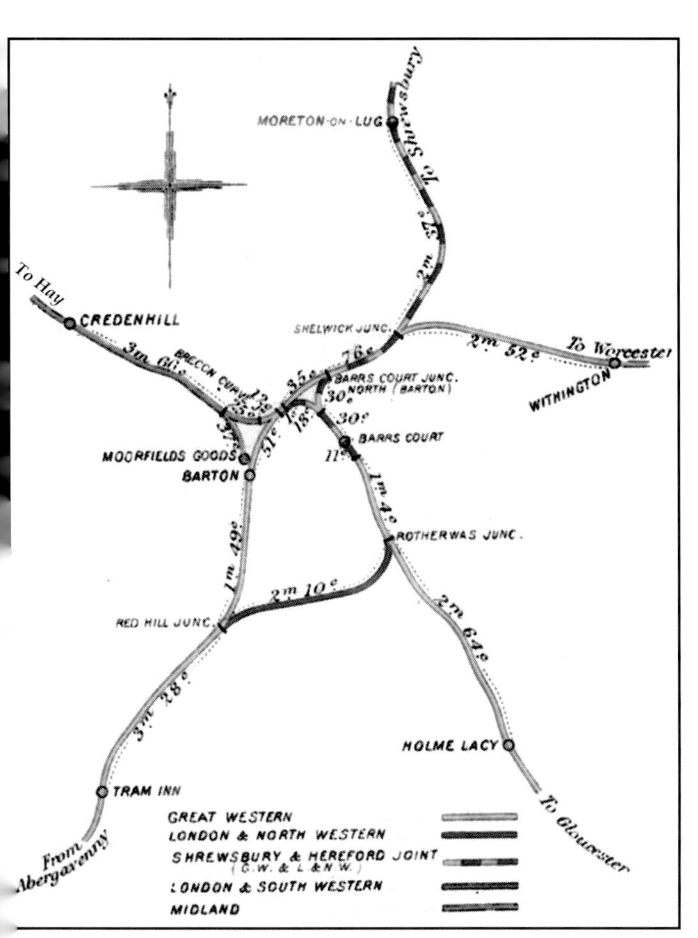

HEREFORD

II. Trains from South Wales (lower left) initially terminated at Barton, while those from the north ended their journeys at Barrs Court. This was also used by services from the Gloucester route, this being broad gauge until 1869. The link line south of the stations was provided in 1866 in an attempt to concentrate traffic on Barrs Court, but this was not to be until 1893, after which time the Barton route was mainly used for freight. To start with, the trains from the Hay line used Barton, but a temporary station at Moorfields was provided from 30th June 1863 until 1st April 1874, when Barton was used again. Eventually the Brecon Curve was completed in 1894 and all passenger trains could use Barrs Court.

1. We start our journey with two views from 6th November 1948. Ex-Lancashire & Yorkshire Railway LMS no. 12428 is arriving at platform 1 with a train from Brecon, which is passing under the staff footbridge linking the two identical goods sheds of 1855. The western one had been for the GWR and the other for the LNWR. (Millbrook House)

The Priory
Highland Cottages
Bridge Inn
Tunnel
College Estate
HEREFORD TRAINING COLLEGE
Ivy Lodge
Newstead
Allotment Gardens
Grand Stand
Meth Ch
Misn. Ch.
Allot Gdns
Saw Mill
Armaddle
WIDEMARSH COMMON
Cricket Ground
Cider Works
Moor House
Widemarsh Brook
Canon Moor Farm
Engine Shed
Goods Sheds
Sports Ground
Brighton Terrace
Station
Stand
Sports Ground
Stone Stand
Hospital
Canal Wharf
MOORFIELDS
CATTLE MARKET
Goods Shed
Cross
Church (Site of)
COMMERCIAL ROAD
Priory (Site of)
Allot Gdns
P A Instn
Isolation Hospital
Eye Hospl
Barton Stn (Goods)
HIGH TOWN
Flour Mill
CATHEDRAL
Deanery
KING ST
CASTLE STREET
Boys Home
Portfield House
CENTRAL AVENUE
Bishop's Palace
Castle Pool
Wye Bridge
Castle Cliff
CASTLE GREEN
Boat Ho.
Bathing Hut
Bishops Meadow (Recreation Ground)
Russian Gun
Victoria Bridge
Wye
Allot Gdns
Territorial Barracks
D

←——— III. The Hay line is on the left and the engine shed within the triangular junction was used by the MR from 1894 to 1924. The goods shed south of it was close to the site of the 1863-74 terminus. Barton station and the GWR engine shed are south of this. The area within the triangle was the site of much railway preservation activity associated with Bulmers Cider. The map is from 1930. Note the extensive sidings provided for the cattle market. Beyond the left border were sidings for an emergency food store in World War II (in use 1942-64) and three for Westfields Cold Store (1941-64). The single line began nearby at Moorfields Junction box, which had a 29-lever frame installed in 1953. It was in use until 24th November 1963; the line to Eardisley closed on 28th September 1964.

2. Having run round and turned, the 2F has propelled its train into platform 4, ready to return to Brecon. A "Hall" class waits to depart with an up main line train. The station had the suffix "Barrs Court" until 1893. (Millbrook House)

3. Ex-GWR no. 2349 waits at the same bay platform ready to leave for Brecon at 12.44pm on 9th September 1949. The 67-lever signal box on the left lasted until 8th June 1973. (H.C.Casserley)

4. The west elevation was photographed in 1962, when its clock was still in place and BR had its own parcels service (right). It was the third station on the site and was completed in 1884. (H.P.White/A.C.Mott coll.)

Other albums to feature Hereford are *Worcester to Hereford* and *Hereford to Newport.*

5. Modernisation had brought LMS and BR class 2 2-6-0s to the Brecon services. Swindon - built no. 46509 is working the 12.42 departure from platform 3 on 13th November 1962, only weeks before cessation of traffic. (P.Chancellor)

WEST OF HEREFORD

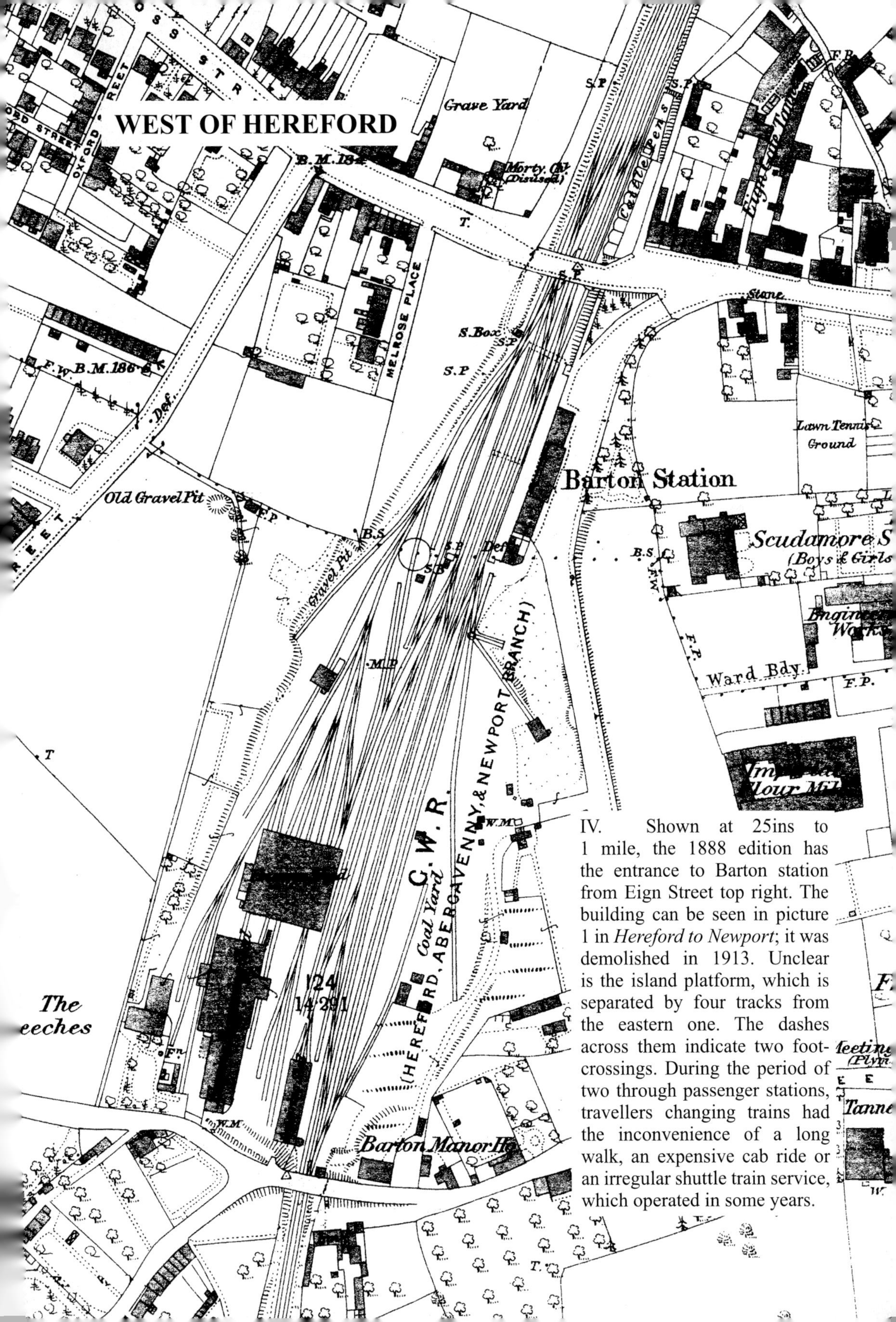

IV. Shown at 25ins to 1 mile, the 1888 edition has the entrance to Barton station from Eign Street top right. The building can be seen in picture 1 in *Hereford to Newport*; it was demolished in 1913. Unclear is the island platform, which is separated by four tracks from the eastern one. The dashes across them indicate two foot-crossings. During the period of two through passenger stations, travellers changing trains had the inconvenience of a long walk, an expensive cab ride or an irregular shuttle train service, which operated in some years.

6. This northward view from 1947 has the Brecon Curve on the right and Barton Goods Depot behind the camera. The straight route was known as "Worcester Mile" and was used by freight trains between the Midlands and South Wales until 1966. The sidings on the left were termed Showyard Sidings, as they were initially used for an agricultural showground. They also served the Hereford Wagon Works and other businesses. Grass covered sidings diverge from them to serve the gasworks and Painter Bros, pylon manufacturers. Langton's timber yard siding was in the centre distance until 1966. Barton & Brecon Curve Junction signal box had 37 levers and stood near the black hut until September 1937. (P.J.Garland/R.S.Carpenter coll.)

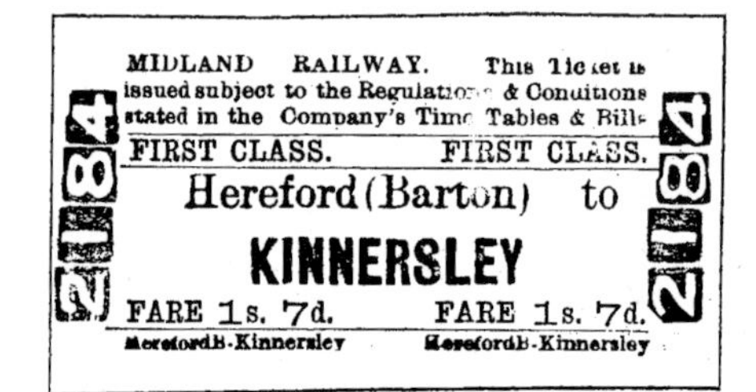

7. We look south at the site of Barton station in 1961, while a coal train stands on the main line. Right of centre is Barton signal box, which closed when traffic southwards ceased in 1966. It continued northwards until 1979. In the right background is the eight-road engine shed and extreme left is the banana warehouse. (S.V.Blencowe/Ted Hancock)

8. A view in the other direction includes the bridge from which picture 7 was taken. Coded 85C, the engine shed was in use until 2nd November 1964. On the northbound goods line on 10th August 1958 is no. 2266, an ex-GWR 0-6-0. The building on the left was the locomotive repair shop. (H.B.Priestley/Milepost 92½)

9. This northward panorama in the 1930s is from the footbridge at the southern apex of the triangle. The line under it was laid by the MR to serve its lengthy goods shed. In the background is its former engine shed, which was used as a store after 1924. This area became the site of Bulmer Railway Centre in 1968; the short-lived terminus had been in the foreground. A 5-ton crane is near the centre. (British Railways)

10. This is the north end of MR's 1892 goods shed. Passengers used the lane in the foreground to reach the temporary MR terminus until the next year. (British Railways)

⟶ V. Bulmer Railway Centre evolved from the cider producer's private siding, where apples had been unloaded since 1955. It was west of the Moorfield Goods Shed shown on map III. The company purchased five Pullman cars in 1968 and adapted them as a cider promotion exhibition and reception centre. An agreement was made that year to lease ex-GWR 4-6-0 no. 6000 *King George V*. The line top right ran to the Brecon Curve and Hereford station. The headshunt on the left was once the route to Hay. At the bottom are the sidings for apple discharge and the exhibition train. Many apples came by train ferry from France. The left diagram indicates the routes existing in 1970 and includes the new locomotive shed. The platforms are shown with shading. The right diagram reveals that a fresh east side to the triangle was laid and a new engine shed was built by 1984. The right curve was known as Priors Curve and the additional platform as Vernons Halt.

11. A 1972 panorama includes much freshly laid track and the stock mentioned earlier. No. 6000 had gained fame by visiting the USA in 1927; it was withdrawn in 1962 after running 2 million miles and became part of the national collection. (R.O.Conway/6000 Locomotive Association)

Below: No. 6000 pioneered the "Return to Steam" in 1972-73, following the total ban on BR. It is in the new shed, seen in the previous picture, in September 1972, receiving attention to its bogie axle boxes following a trip to Old Oak Common. The bell was bestowed on it in the USA. (Derek Evans FRPS FRSA)

12. Backing onto the Bulmer Pullmans on 2nd October 1976 is ex-LMS 4-6-2 no. 6201 *Princess Elizabeth*. To the left of the rear coaches is the former goods shed and to the right are the access steps and the apple discharge pit. Locomotive societies based here included Princess Elizabeth (from 1976), Merchant Navy (from 1975) and Worcester, from the outset. (T.Heavyside)

13. Much other stock came to the site and seen on 14th March 1981 are Peckett no. 1579 *Pectin* of 1955 and Hunslet 0-6-0ST no. 3793 *Shropshire* of 1953. Sadly, closure of the premises came on 31st May 1993. (T.Heavyside)

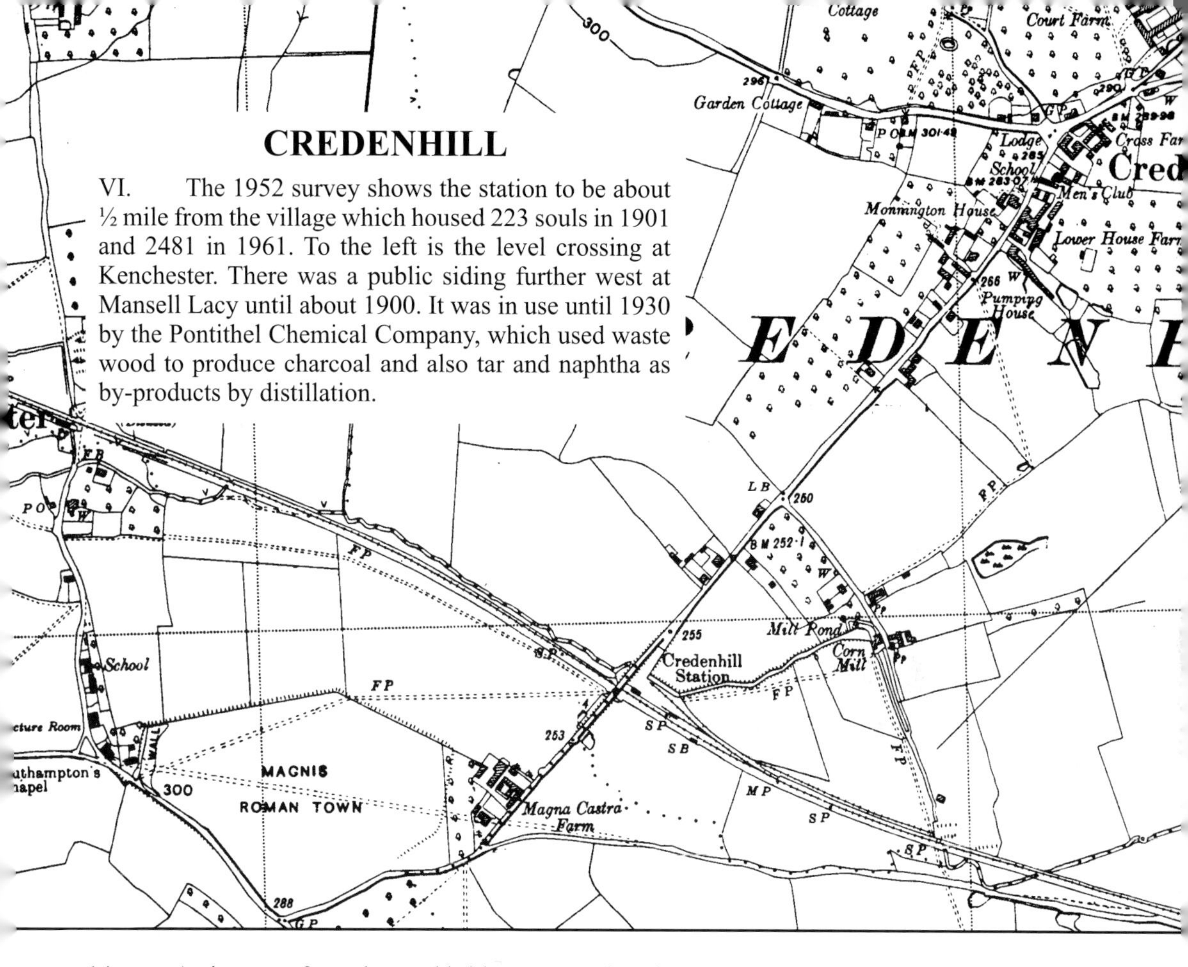

CREDENHILL

VI. The 1952 survey shows the station to be about ½ mile from the village which housed 223 souls in 1901 and 2481 in 1961. To the left is the level crossing at Kenchester. There was a public siding further west at Mansell Lacy until about 1900. It was in use until 1930 by the Pontithel Chemical Company, which used waste wood to produce charcoal and also tar and naphtha as by-products by distillation.

14. A view east from the road bridge was produced on a postcard in about 1910. A large item of equipment is at the end-loading dock. The signal box had 28 levers, although many were not used. (Lens of Sutton coll.)

15. The old coach body was still in place when 2-6-0 no. 46523 called with the 10.25am from Brecon on 7th July 1959. No goods shed was provided, unlike the next two stations, but freight was handled here until 28th September 1964. (SLS coll.)

→

16. The signal box was closed in 1929 and soon demolished. Six sidings had been laid down beyond it in World War I to serve a depot acting as an outpost of the Royal Ordnance Factory at Rotherwas, south of Hereford. They were in use in 1917-27. (Lens of Sutton coll.)

→

17. The station was staffed part time only from 1955, but was well maintained to the end. It became the site of the village sports club and community centre. (Lens of Sutton coll.)

CREDENHILL
CREDENHILL

WESTMOOR FLAG STATION

18. This was a private station built by a local landowner. The public stations on the route were mostly of timber construction, but no expense was spared on this one. The platform was for just one coach. (Mowat coll./Brunel University))

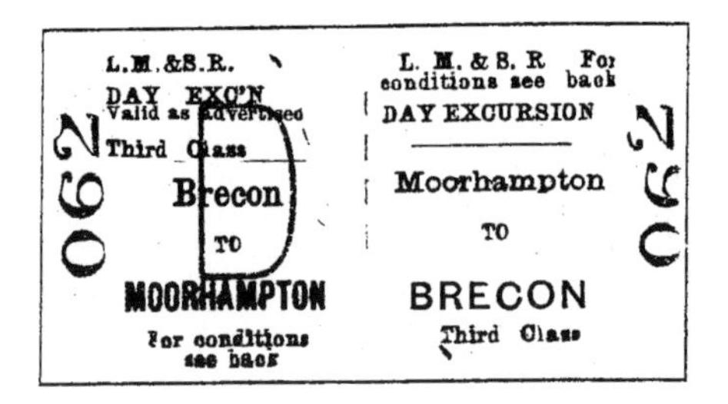

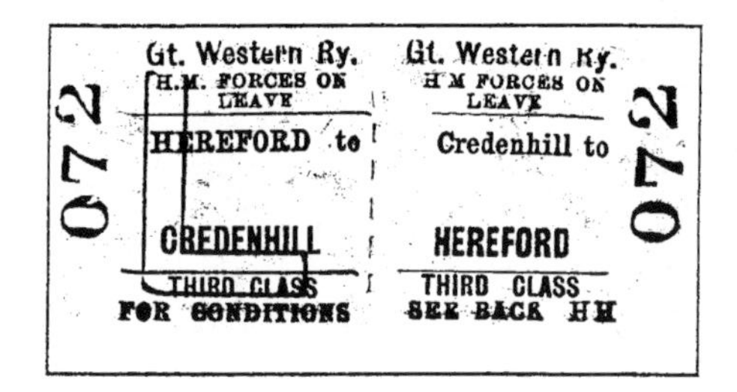

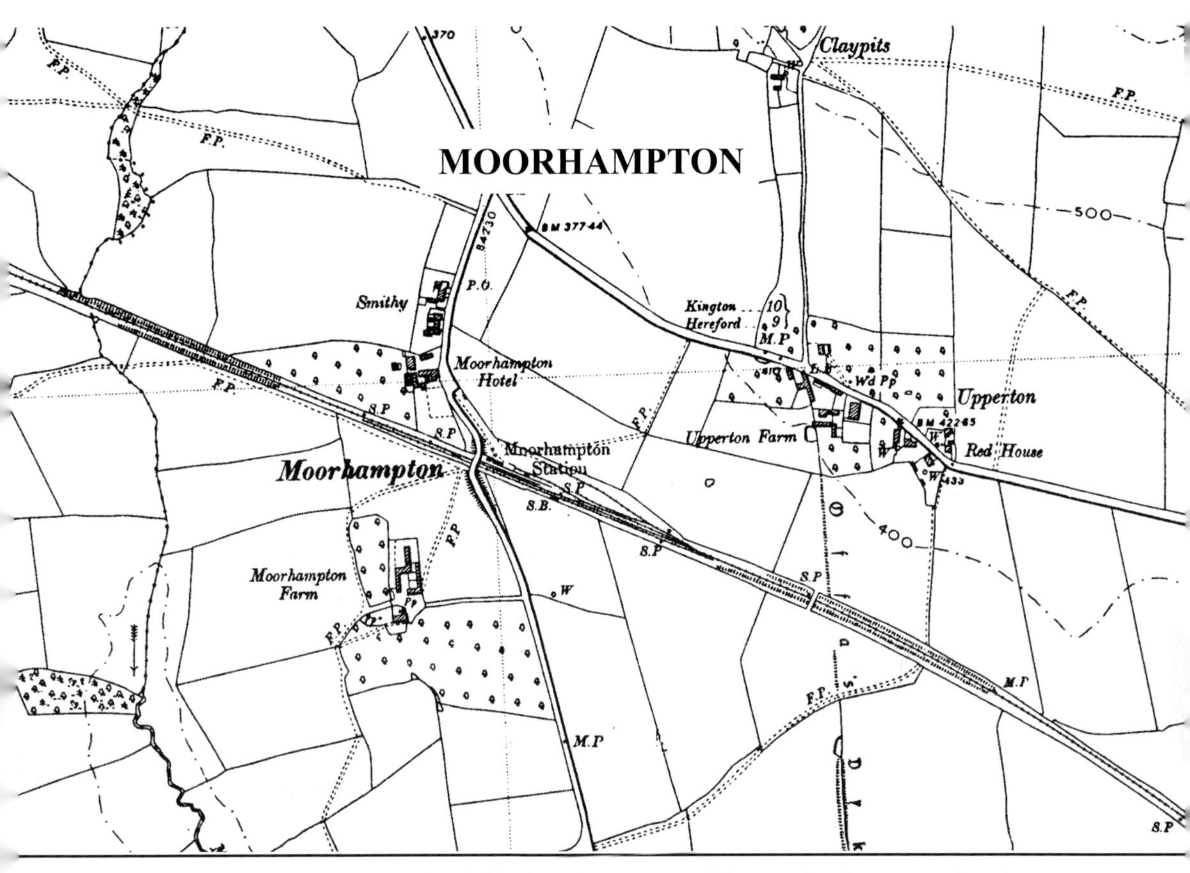

VII. This was a thinly populated district, the name applying to the few properties shown on this 1952 extract. Timber was loaded here from a 2ft gauge tramway in the period 1943-46.

19. There was likely to have been one stationmaster, two clerks and two signalmen, the others being porters. The unroofed section was for gentlemen. (Lens of Sutton coll.)

20. Evident in this view towards Hereford is the parcel weighing machine and the goods shed. The 1892 signal box had a 24-lever frame; the box had been raised up in 1914. (Lens of Sutton coll.)

21. Approaching from the west on 23rd April 1958 is BR class 2 2-6-0 no. 78004. The tanks are probably empty from Dowlais Steelworks or the ICI ammonia plant near there. Note the small signal arm for up goods trains to enter the loop. (H.C.Casserley)

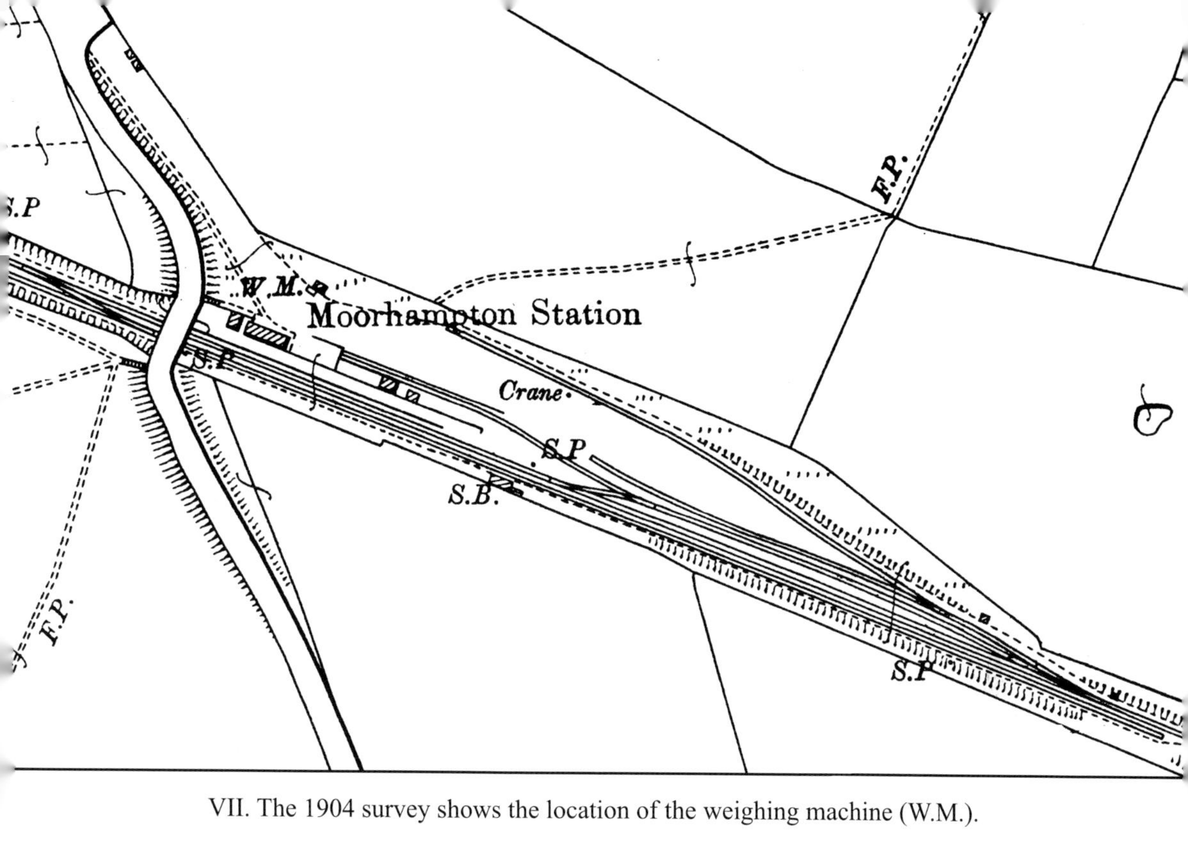

VII. The 1904 survey shows the location of the weighing machine (W.M.).

22. The station was manned for only one shift from December 1955. With only one platform, it was not possible to pass passenger trains here normally. The west end of the loop is seen on the same day. (R.M.Casserley)

23. Also on the same day, we witness the departure of a train for Hereford and that goods traffic is still present. The small shed was the lamp room and the larger one was for the permanent way trolley, hence the boards in the track. (R.M.Casserley)

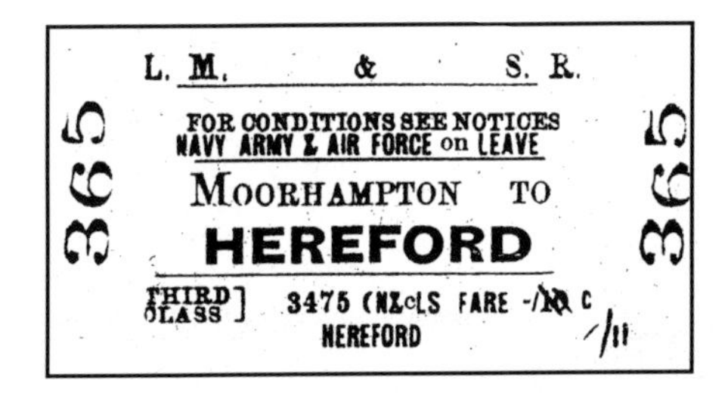

24. Although the sidings are not visible, they were officially in use until withdrawal of passenger service. In the background is the crane, which was of 5-ton capacity. Westbound is ex-GWR 0-6-0PT no. 4635, but no date was recorded. (SLS coll.)

25. The final picture is from July 1964, only two months before all traffic ceased. The post once carried a tablet catcher for single line operation. The site was later used by the Caravan Club. (M.A.King)

KINNERSLEY

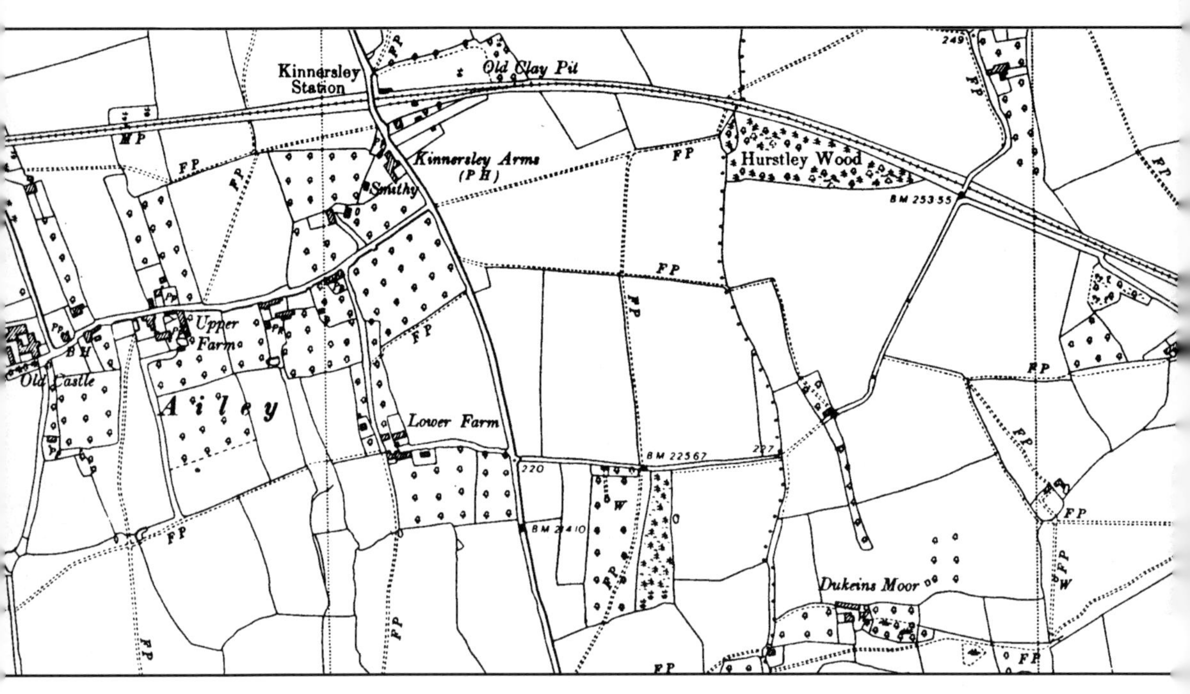

VIII. Few dwellings but many orchards typify this area. About one mile north of the station is the scattered village, which housed 200-250 folk during the life of the line. This is the 1952 edition.

26. A 1932 view towards Hereford shows that the small goods shed was remote from the platform, unlike Moorhampton. (P.Q.Treloar coll.)

27. “Dean Goods” no. 2541 was photographed on 24th March 1951 with a Hereford to Brecon pick-up goods. Ex-GWR locos were then gradually ousting the ex-Lancashire & Yorkshire 0-6-0s used by the LMS on the route for many years. (P.M.Alexander/P.Q.Treloar coll.)

28. The passenger’s approach path is on the left in this April 1958 record of the south elevation and Mr. Casserley’s faithful Hillman 10, by then over 20 years old. (H.C.Casserley)

29. Meanwhile, Mr. Casserley Junior was extending the survey and making it clear that gentlemen were provided with a separate building at this station. (R.M.Casserley)

30. This fine panorama is sadly without a date, but the locomotive is 0-6-0 no. 2280, a type introduced by the GWR in 1930. (SLS coll.)

31. The smart enamel signs were provided in the early days of BR, but the lanterns were probably nearly a century old. The cattle dock is included in this 1962 photograph. (Lens of Sutton coll.)

32. Goods and passenger services were both withdrawn at the end of 1962. By 30th July 1964, little had changed, apart from grass and weeds growing where practical. (M.A.King)

South from Titley Junction

TITLEY JUNCTION

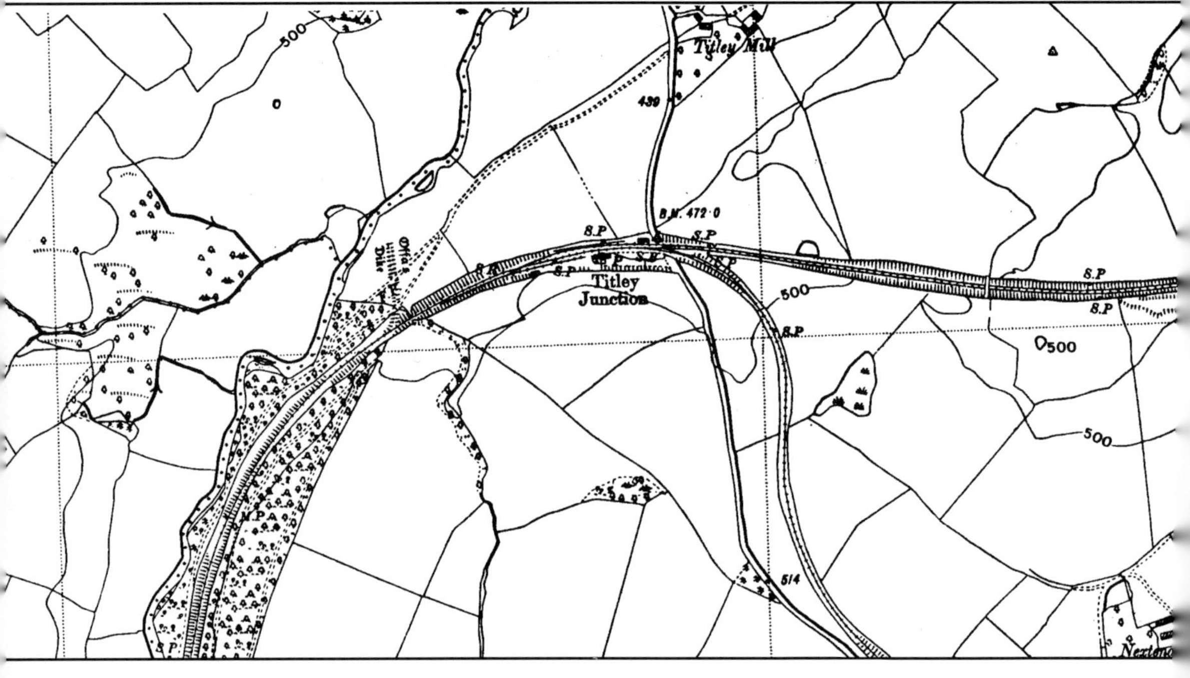

IX. The Leominster-New Radnor line runs from right to left across this 1948 map. Branching from it is the Kington & Eardisley Railway of 1874, which was operated by the GWR.

KINGTON and EARDISLEY.—Great Western.

Fm. Brecon & Hereford, 198.	gov	mrn	aft	aft				
Eardisley ....dep	8 20	1145	4 15	7 2	....	....	....	....
Almeley	8 25	1155	4 20	7 7	....	....	....	....
Lyon's Hall	8 40	1212	4 35	7 20	....	....	....	....
Titley	8 45	1220	4 40	7 40	....	....	....	....
Kington.............arr	8 50	1223	4 45	7 45	....	....	....	....

Down.	mrn	gov	aft	aft				
Kington ....dep	....	9 20	3 30	6 25	....	....	....	....
Titley	7 25	9 25	3 35	6 30	....	....	....	....
Lyon's Hall	7 40	9 30	3 40	6 35	....	....	....	....
Almeley	7 57	9 40	3 50	6 45	....	....	....	....
Eardisley 198 ....arr	8 5	9 45	3 55	6 50	....	....	....	....

June 1876

KINGTON and EARDISLEY.—Great Western.

Miles.	Down.	Week Days only.								
		mrn		aft		aft				
	Kington .....dep.	9 10	....	3 25	....	6 28	....	....	....	....
1¾	Titley	9 15	....	3 30	....	6 33	....	....	....	....
3¾	Lyonshall	9 21	....	3 36	....	6 39	....	....	....	....
6½	Almeley	9 32	....	3 49	....	6 48	....	....	....	....
8¾	Eardisley 678 arr	9 38	....	3 57	....	6 53	....	....	....	....

Miles.	Up.	Week Days only.								
		mrn		aft		aft				
	Eardisley ....dep.	9 57	....	4 30	....	7 10	....	....	....	....
2¼	Almeley	10 2	....	4 35	....	7 17	....	....	....	....
5¼	Lyonshall	1013	....	4 46	....	7 29	....	....	....	....
7	Titley	1018	....	4 51	....	7 35	....	....	....	....
8¾	Kington ......arr.	1022	....	4 55	....	7 39	....	....	....	....

August 1916

KINGTON, EARDISLEY, and PRESTEIGN.

Miles.	Down.	Week Days only.							
		mrn	mrn	mrn		aft	aft		aft
	Kington..........dep.	9 0	1029	1117	..	1 15	3 30	..	5 23
1¾	Titley (above)......arr.	9 4	1032	1121	..	1 19	3 34	..	5 27
—	Titley..........dep.	9 5	..	1122	..	..	3 35	..	..
3¼	Lyonshall	9 10	..	1126	..	..	3 40	..	..
6½	Almeley............	9 25	..	1134	..	..	3 55	..	..
8¾	Eardisley 699 ..arr.	9 38	..	1139	..	..	4 5	..	..
—	Titley ....dep.	..	1033	..	..	1 22	..	..	5 33
3¼	Forge Crossing Halt...	..	1036	..	..	1 27	..	..	5 38
7¼	Presteign ....arr.	..	1045	..	..	1 38	..	..	5 49

Miles.	Up.	Week Days only.							
		mrn	mrn	non		aft	aft	aft	
	Presteign ....dep.	..	1051	..	..	2 38	..	6 3	..
4	Forge Crossing Halt...	..	11 0	..	..	2 48	..	6 13	..
5¼	Titley (above).....arr.	..	11 3	..	..	2 54	..	6 19	..
—	Mls Eardisley.....dep.	10 2	..	12 0	..	..	4 48	..	..
—	2¼ Almeley	10 7	..	12 6	..	..	4 53	..	..
—	5½ Lyonshall..........	1014	..	1215	..	..	5 1	..	..
—	7 Titley (above).arr.	1017	..	1221	..	..	5 5	..	..
—	Titley ....dep.	1018	11 4	1222	..	2 59	5 6	6 20	..
7¼	Kington..........arr.	1022	11 7	1226	..	3 3	5 9	6 24	..

August 1939

33. Two photographs from 1959 give a comprehensive record of the station, which had lost its passenger service on 7th February 1955, long before Dr. Beeching sharpened his axe. (J.Moss/R.S.Carpenter coll.)

IX. About half the length of the headshunt is shown on the left of this 1903 extract.

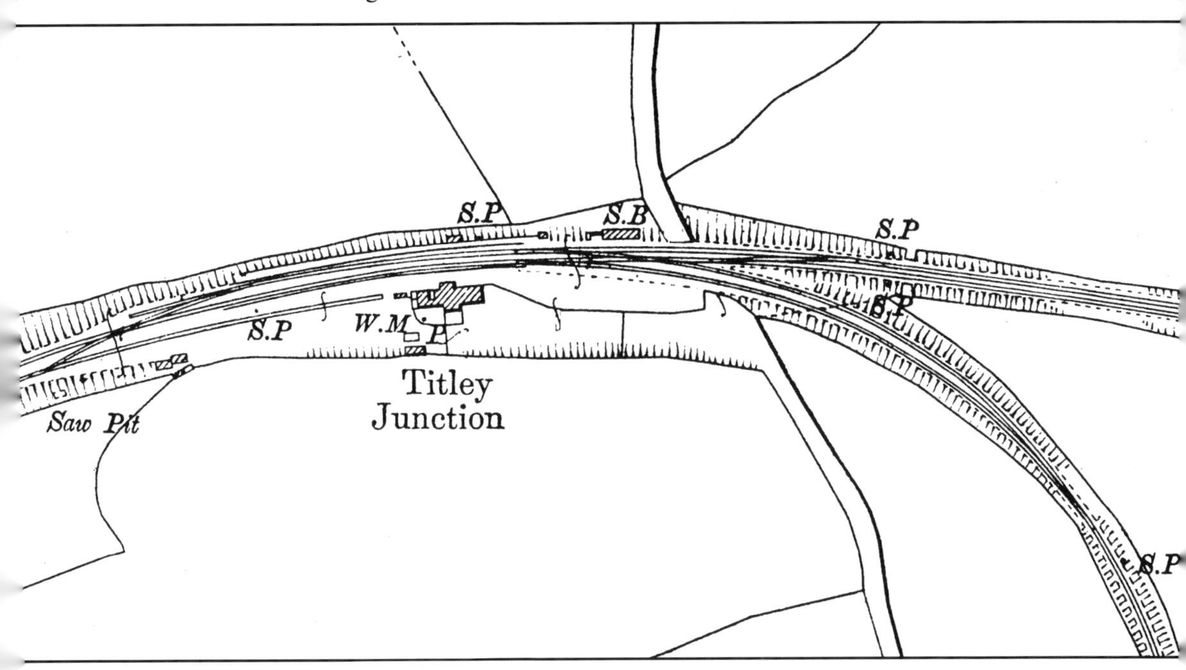

34. The line to Eardisley had branched off in the distance until 1940, but surprisingly the up starting signal still carried a route indicator in 1959. Trains from both Eardisley and Presteign ran through to Kington, none terminating here. The same train for long served both branches. One of the two points for Eardisley trains remains. (J.Moss/R.S.Carpenter coll.)

→ 35. Freight continued to Kington until 28th September 1964, but the service ceased here on 6th July 1959. The route to Eardisley climbed over a steep ridge, about three miles of it being on a gradient of around 1 in 45. This signal box was in use from 1902 until 1958. (J.Moss/R.S.Carpenter coll.)

LYONSHALL

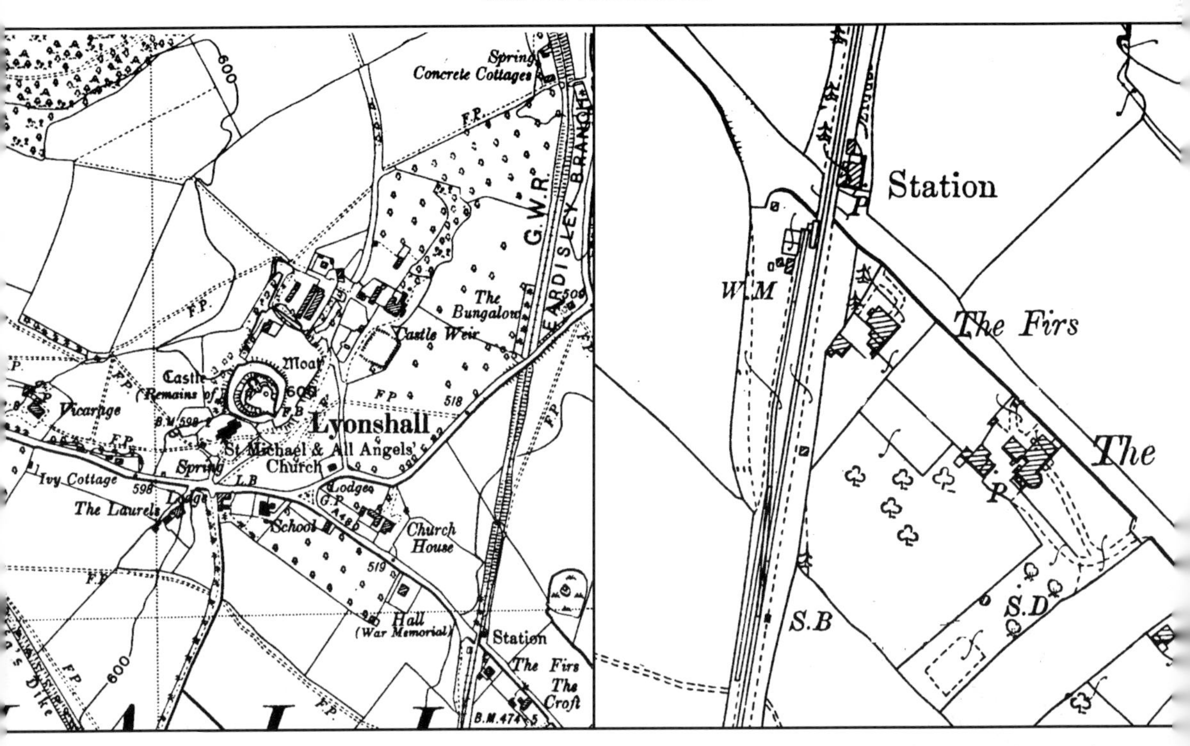

X. The 1948 editions still shows the station and its single siding in place, despite total closure of the line on 1st July 1940. The siding had been converted to a loop in 1928.

36. This view south across the bridge over the road is towards the small goods yard in about 1932. The summit of the line was in this vicinity, at around 500ft above sea level. (Postcard)

ALMELEY

XI. The road to the nearby village is on the right of this 1903 map.

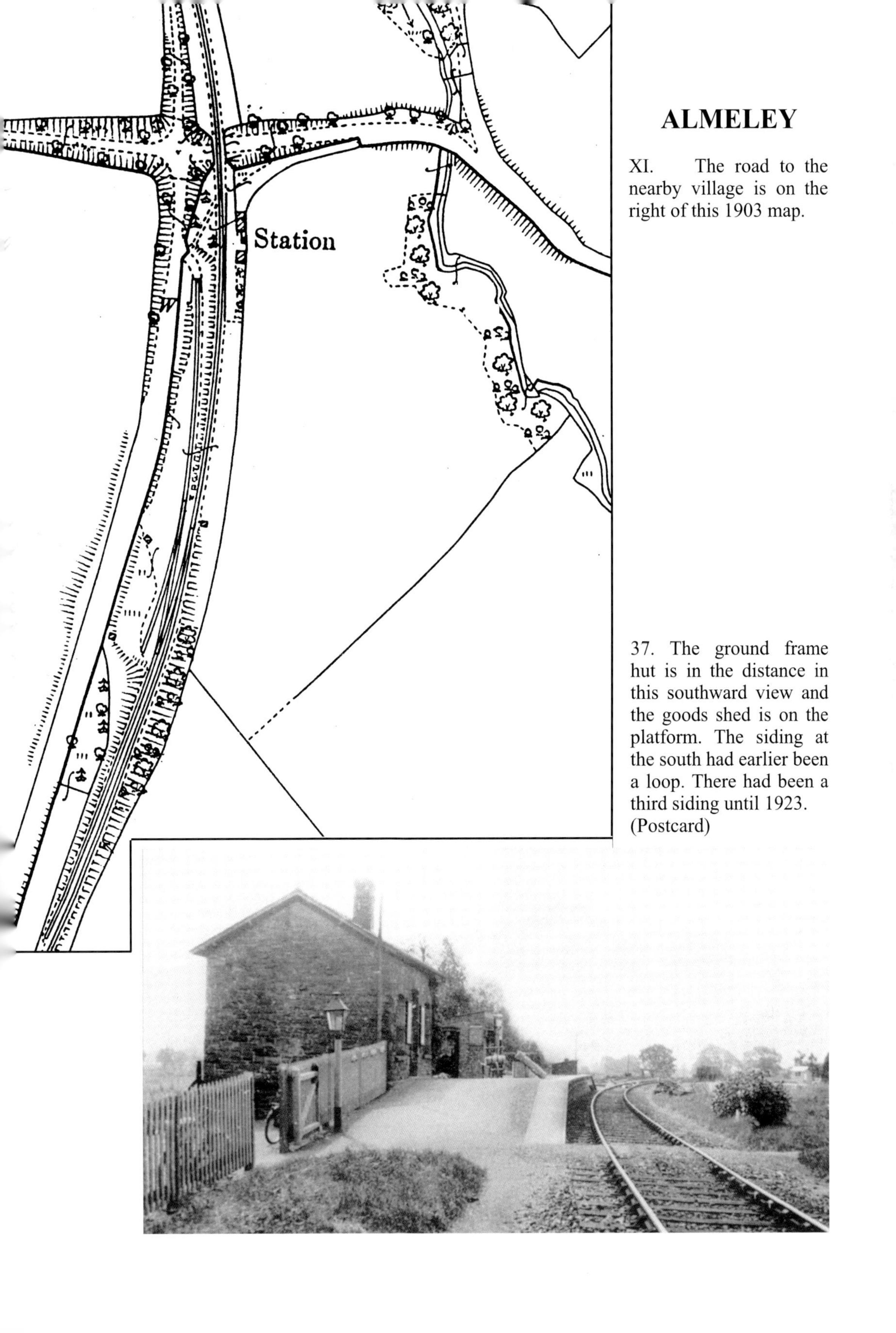

37. The ground frame hut is in the distance in this southward view and the goods shed is on the platform. The siding at the south had earlier been a loop. There had been a third siding until 1923. (Postcard)

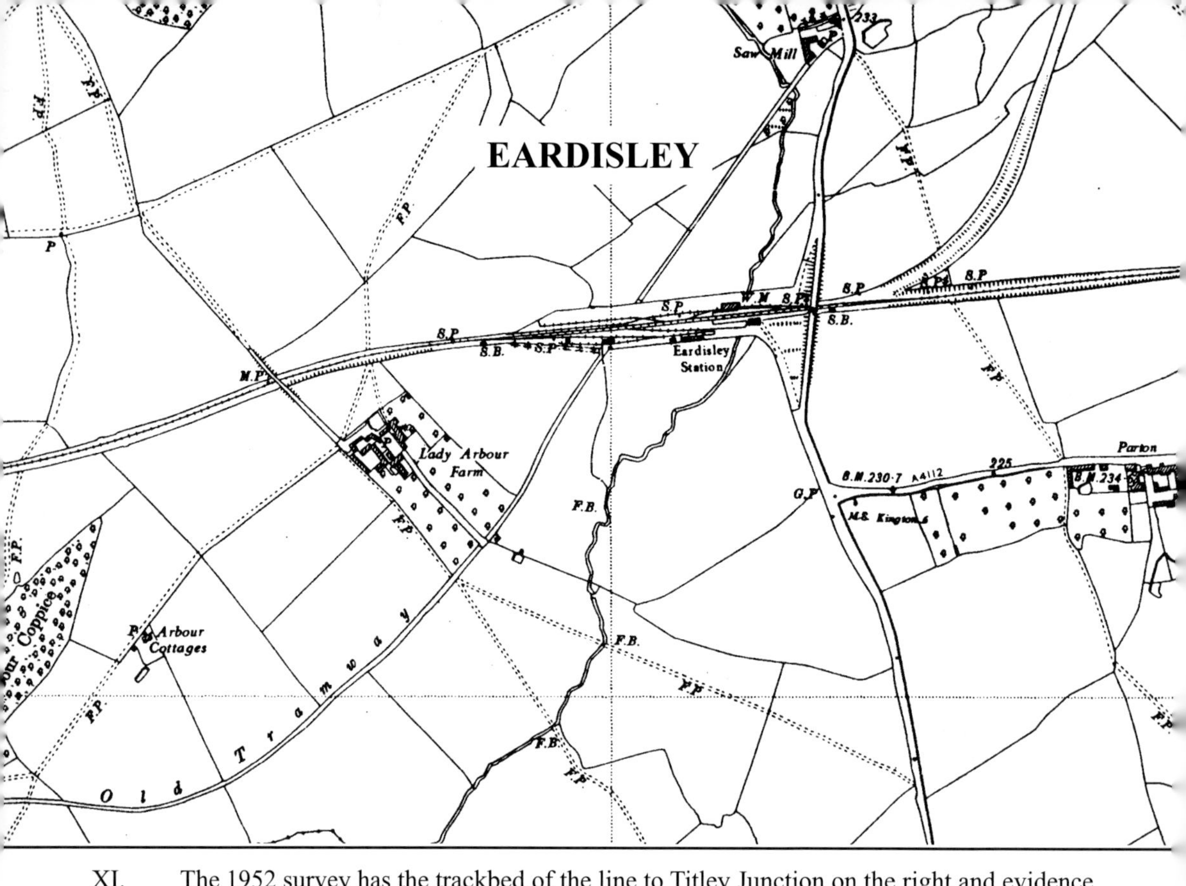

XI. The 1952 survey has the trackbed of the line to Titley Junction on the right and evidence of the earlier tramway route to Kington on the left.

38. The bridge made a good vantage point for the photographer to record the staff and a train from Kington. The class 517 0-4-2T has run round its train, probably seen in the late 1880s. (R.S.Carpenter coll.)

39. Recorded in the Summer of 1910, class 1076 0-6-0ST no. 1137 stands with a train for Kington. The ballast seems very poor. (G.M.Perkins/R.S.Carpenter coll.)

40. A train arrives for Hereford on 15th September 1949. West Box had been in the distance until about 1925. No. 2349 has an improvised smokebox number. (SLS coll.)

41. A train for Brecon departs in about 1948 behind 0-6-0 no. 2349 and the panorama gives us an opportunity to see much of the goods yard. (D.K.Jones coll.)

42. A goods train bound for Hereford is held in the up platform on 13th September 1956. It had been waiting for the down passenger service from which this picture was taken. (R.M.Casserley)

43. Eardisley Junction signal box was at the east end of the loop and is seen on 29th April 1958. A section of the line to Titley Junction was relaid (left) during World War II to serve a Ministry of Works siding. It ran to a private siding for a timber company from September 1953 until April 1956. (H.C.Casserley)

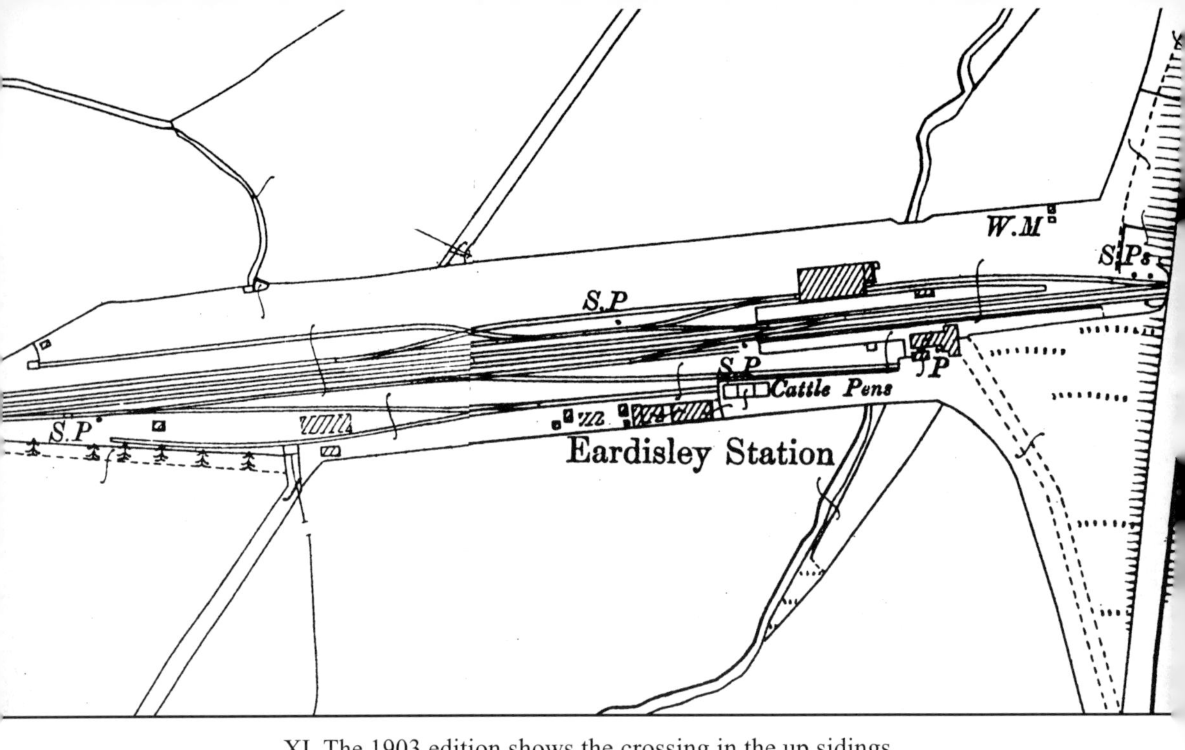

XI. The 1903 edition shows the crossing in the up sidings.

44. We now have two photographs from 3rd April 1961, both taken from the bridge. The curve seen in the last picture has gone. The box was listed as having 35 levers, plus two double wire levers installed in 1934. (J.Langford)

45. With residual snow evident, the goods shed loop seems neglected. Part time staffing was introduced in November 1960. The goods shed remained when the area was developed as an industrial estate. (J.Langford)

46. Class 2 2-6-0 no. 46514 enters the down loop on 8th August 1962, the last year of passenger trains. The train is the 12.45pm from Hereford to Brecon. (R.A.Lumber/D.H.Mitchell coll.)

47. Photographed on the same day was no. 78004 with an up goods train at 1.0pm. The yard remained open until 28th September 1964, although goods traffic westwards had ceased on 4th May of that year. (R.A.Lumber/D.H.Mitchell coll.)

48. Our final view is also from 1962 and features the timber built structures which were dismantled for rebuilding as the Welshpool & Llanfair Railway's eastern terminus at Raven Square. (Lens of Sutton coll.)

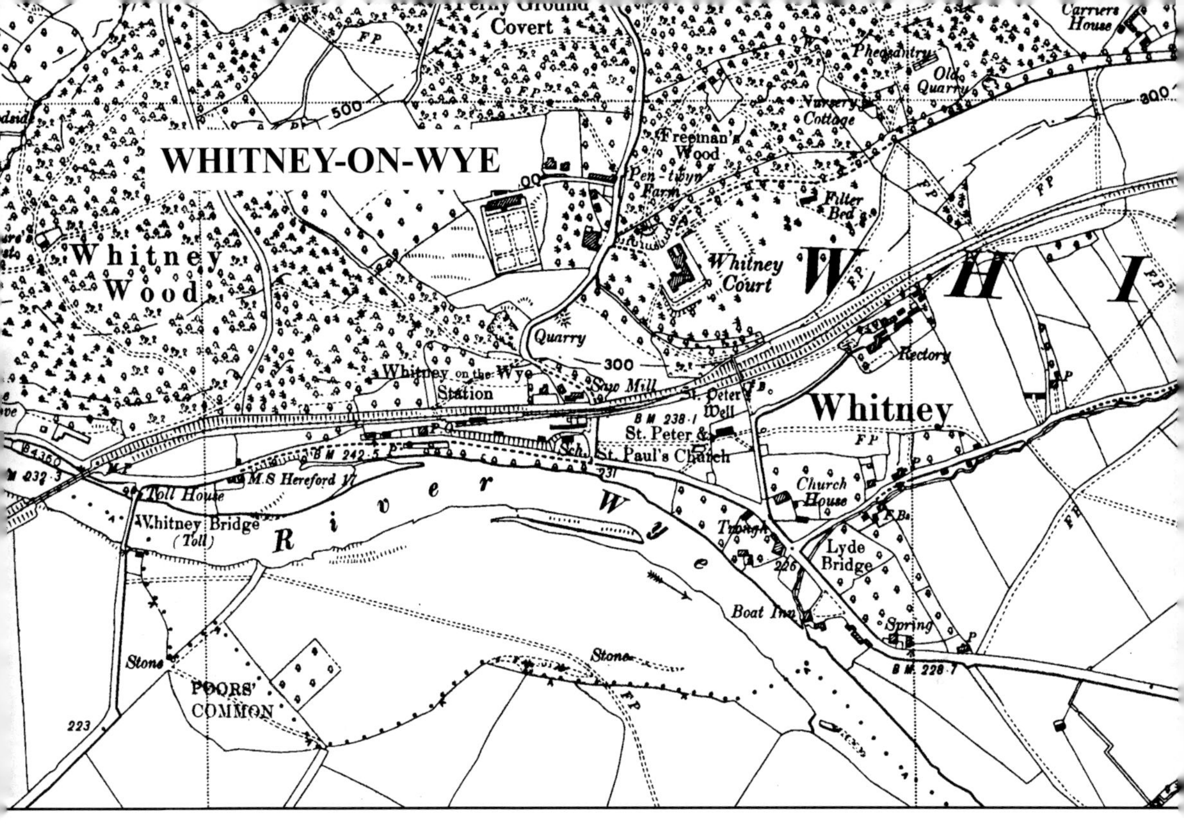

XII. The 1952 edition shows the name of the station as used from 1880 to 1924. The population was 270 in 1901 and 137 in 1961. The Wyc bridge (left) was closed for two weeks in December 1961, due to flood damage.

49. A postcard from about 1910 appears to include two passengers, two members of staff and one telegraph pole. The pole route was north of the track. There had been a signal box until 1892. (R.S.Carpenter coll.)

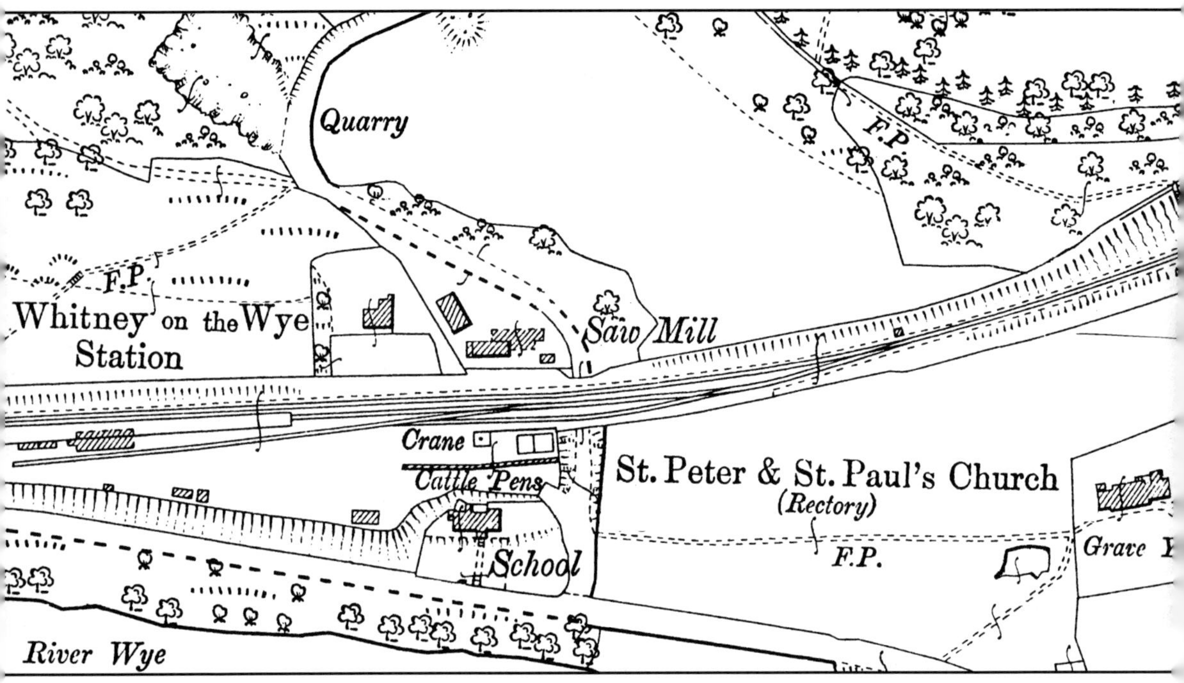

XII. The 1903 survey shows more clearly that there was a road between the saw mill and the goods yard, under the railway.

50. A 1932 record includes the euphemism CLOAK ROOM for the parcels shed and also the pre-1924 name on the board. Part of the goods yard is in the distance; it had a 30-cwt crane. (R.M.Casserley coll.)

51. No. 46520 runs in from Hereford, the revised name having been applied to the MR-style fencing. The LMS introduced this type of 2-6-0 in 1946. (SLS coll.)

52. The prospective passengers' perspective is pictured on 21st August 1961, with the long siding showing signs of neglect. The yard closed at the end of 1962. (Lens of Sutton coll.)

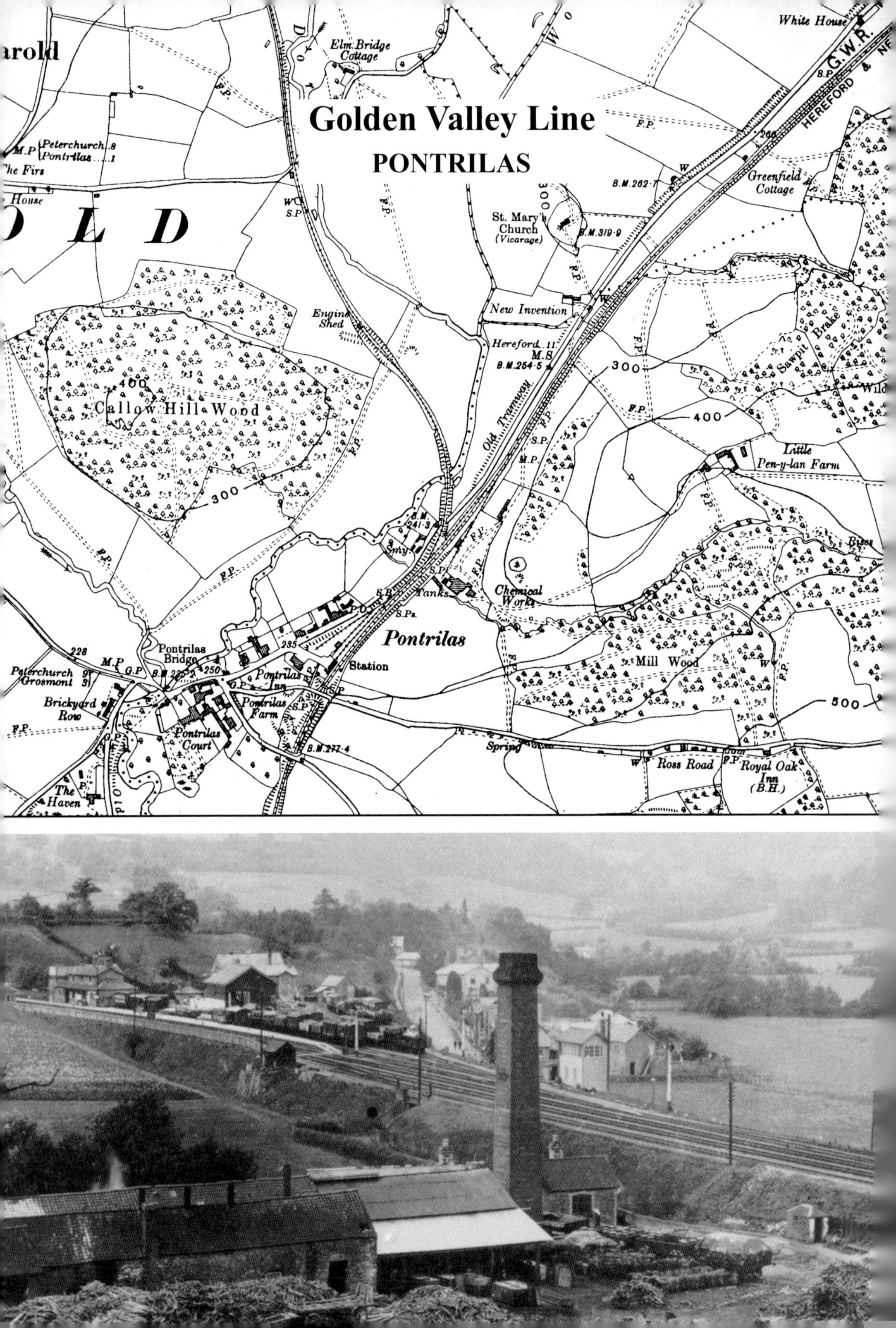
Golden Valley Line
PONTRILAS
White House
G.W.R.
HEREFORD
Elm Bridge Cottage
Peterchurch 8
Pontrilas 1
The Firs
House
Greenfield Cottage
St. Mary's Church
(Vicarage)
B.M. 319·9
B.M. 262·7
New Invention
Engine Shed
Hereford 11
B.M. 254·5
Old Tramway
Sawpit Brake
Callow Hill Wood
Little Pen-y-lan Farm
Chemical Works
Tanks
Pontrilas
Station
Mill Wood
Pontrilas Bridge
Peterchurch 9
Grosmont 3
Brickyard Row
Pontrilas Inn
Pontrilas Farm
Pontrilas Court
The Haven
B.M. 277·4
Spring
Ross Road
Royal Oak Inn
(B.H.)
300
400
500

← XIII. The main line is top right and close to it is evidence of the 1829 horse-worked Hereford Railway, plus a church with no road access. The map is from 1922.

← 53. In the foreground is the Pontrilas chemical works, with four wagons standing in its siding, which was in use from 1879 until 1929. The wood was used to produce a variety of liquid compounds, plus vast quantities of charcoal. (Lens of Sutton coll.)

54. A typical Golden Valley mixed train has arrived in the bay and passengers await a main line service. The large tank was for locomotive water, the small one being added for domestic purposes when mains arrived. The branch descends at 1 in 55 and passes over the bridges in the background. (R.S.Carpenter coll.)

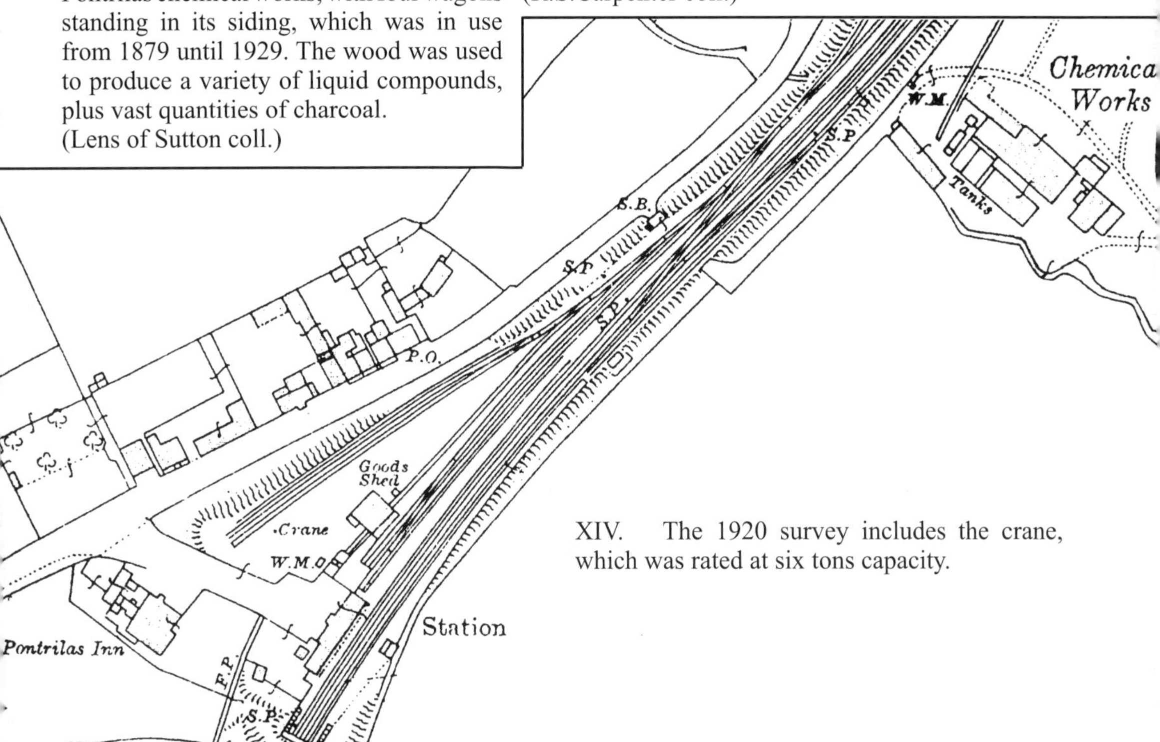

XIV. The 1920 survey includes the crane, which was rated at six tons capacity.

55. The tail of another mixed train stands in the bay as we gaze at the 37yd-long tunnel under a ridge of land at the western tip of which is the village. The photograph is from about 1923, by which time the main canopy had been extended. (Stations UK)

Other views can be seen in pictures 37 to 44 in our *Hereford to Newport* album.

56. It is 1st August 1956 and 0-4-2T no. 5818 has assembled its goods train for the branch. Pontrilas lost its passenger service on 9th June 1958 and its goods yard on 12th October 1964. The main building was still standing in 2006 and the signal box was still in use, as was the up loop. (P.J.Garland/R.S.Carpenter coll.)

NORTH OF PONTRILAS

57. The shed was remote from the station (see map), presumably because there was little spare space near the station. Seen in 1909 is 517 class 0-4-2T no. 1437. (G.M.Perkins/R.S.Carpenter coll.)

58. This view of the 1881 structure is from 1948. A steam pump for filling the water tank was provided at the far end of the shed, which was in use until 2nd February 1953. Thereafter, the engine came from Hereford, with a pick-up goods. It was usually a 5800 class 0-4-2T, previously outstationed from Pontypool Road shed. (R.M.Casserley coll.)

59. Two photographs from April 1961 show the connection to the munition stores from the branch, which was only a residual stub by that time. (J.Langford)

60. The stores were established by the Royal Ordnance Factory in 1941, so that its products were kept at a remote location, away from the production site which was south of Hereford. The guard room is adjacent to the bridge over the River Dore. (J.Langford)

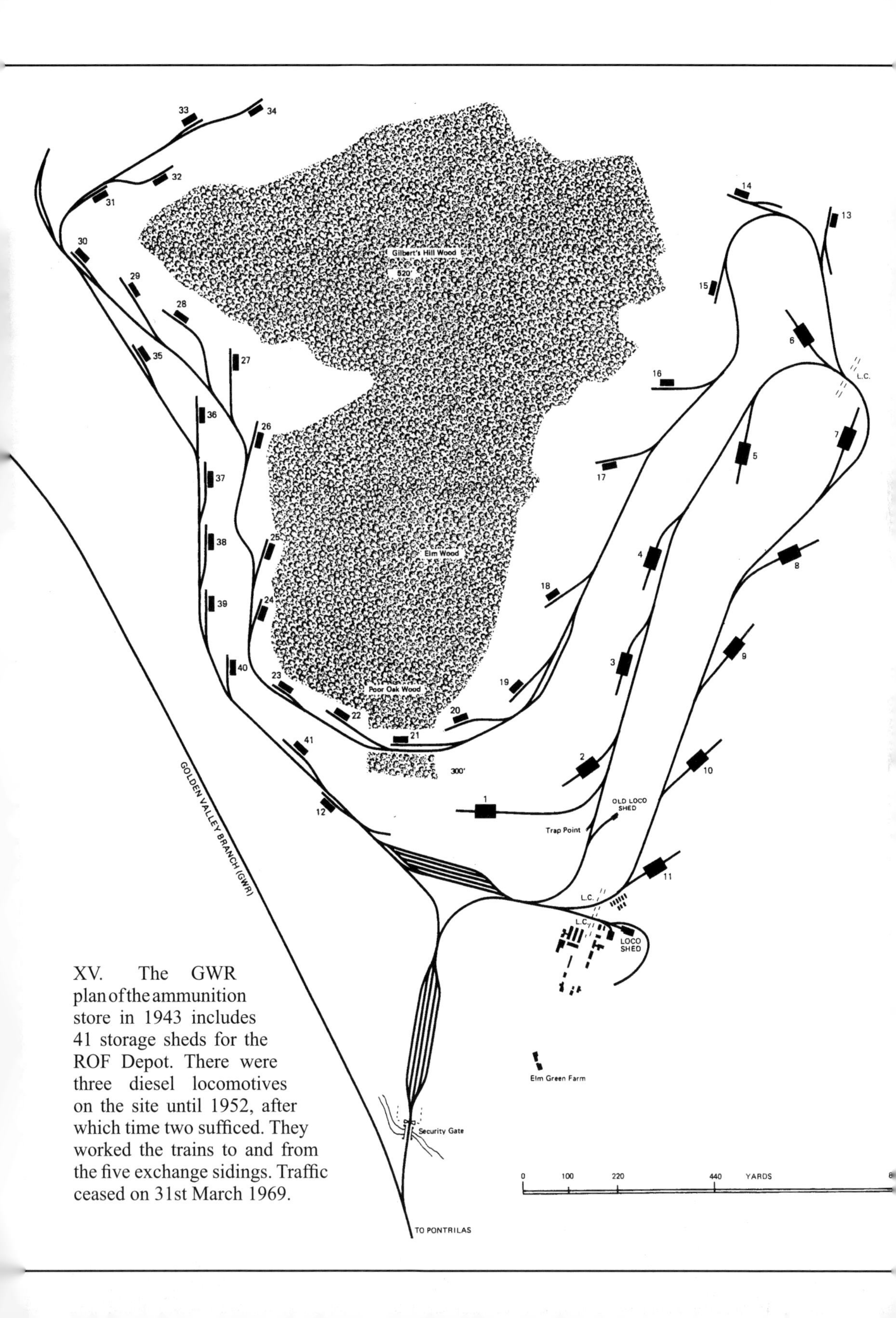

XV. The GWR plan of the ammunition store in 1943 includes 41 storage sheds for the ROF Depot. There were three diesel locomotives on the site until 1952, after which time two sufficed. They worked the trains to and from the five exchange sidings. Traffic ceased on 31st March 1969.

ABBEYDORE

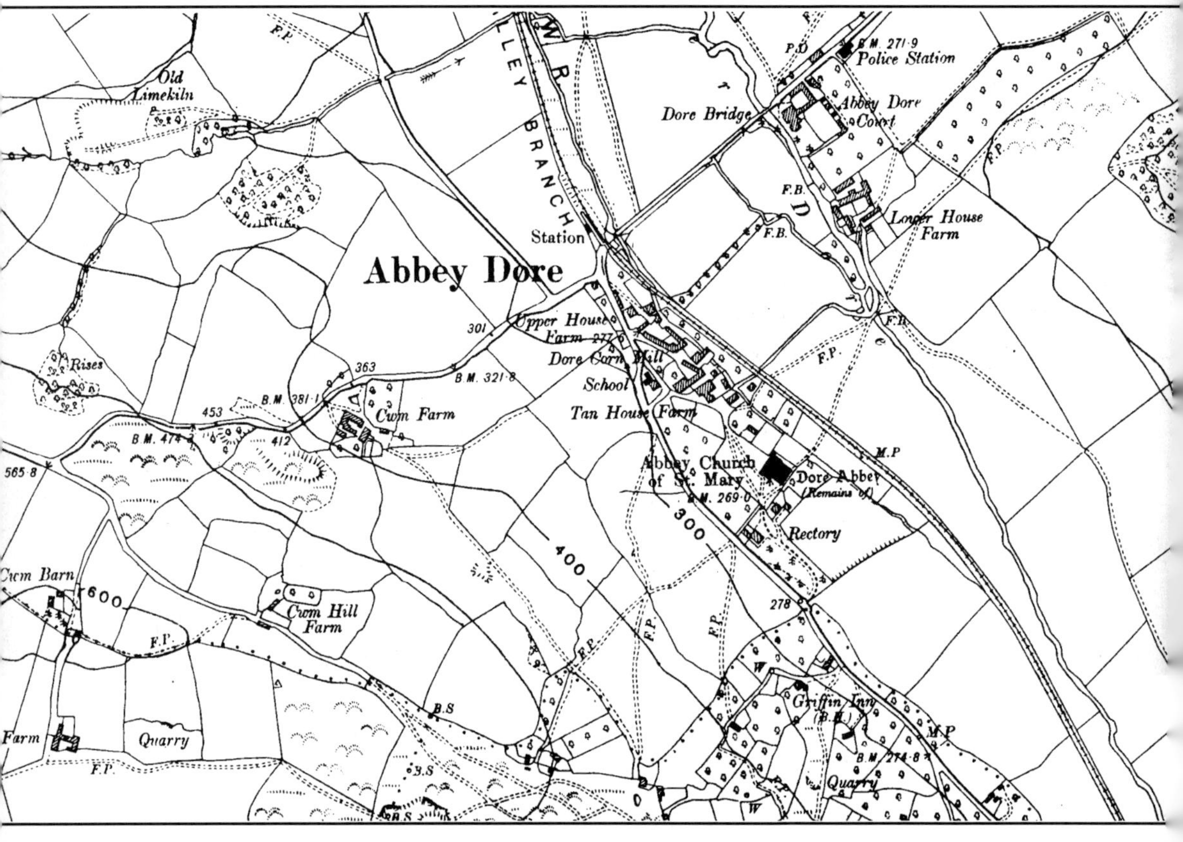

XVI. The 1922 edition reveals that only the church remained of the ancient abbey. It was visible from the platform. There were 456 residents in 1901, but the figure declined greatly.

61. The east elevation was recorded in the 1930s. There was a staff of three in 1929-31 and two for the remainder of the decade. (Lens of Sutton coll.)

62. A northward view from May 1950 includes all of the goods loop and the brake van about to be reattached to the short train bound for Dorstone, by then the "head of steel". (R.G.Nelson/T.Walsh coll.)

XVI. The 1904 survey shows a weighing machine to be present.

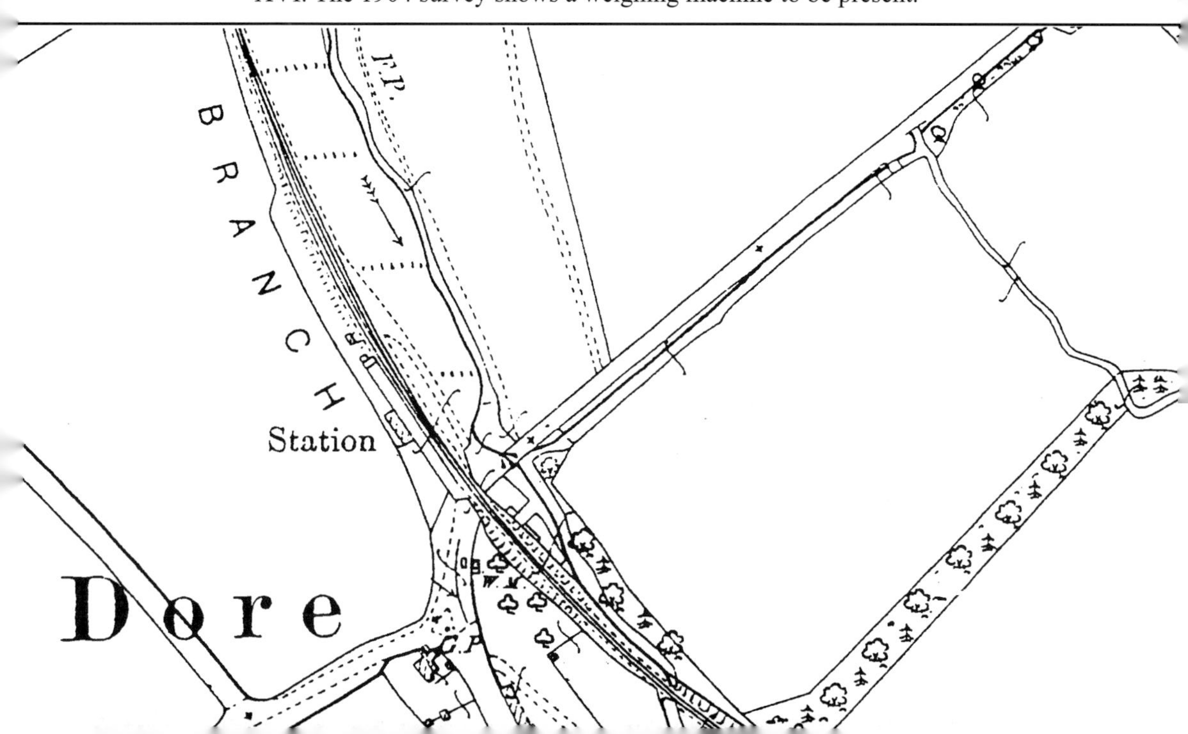

63. Traffic was much heavier on 21st June 1951; the locomotive is 0-4-2T no. 5818. The vans were for the Ordnance Store, but they had to be taken to the end of the line first to avoid shunting in the exchange sidings. (SLS coll.)

Abbeydore	**1903**	**1913**	**1923**	**1932**
Passenger tickets issued	6413	3352	2919	1155
Season tickets issued	*	*	3	-
Parcels forwarded	423	617	891	987
General goods forwarded (tons)	636	404	2321	533
Coal and coke received (tons)	421	403	361	125
Other minerals received (tons)	949	630	371	157
General goods received (tons)	339	454	447	522
Trucks of livestock handled	3	14	13	43

(* not available.)

64. The Hillman reveals the identity of the photographer recording the ground frame details for posterity on 23rd April 1958. It was unlocked by a key attached to the single line token. One of the levers worked the facing point lock. (H.C.Casserley)

65. Three more photographs that day complete our survey of the scene. This includes remnants of the cattle pen, the catch point rod (the other end is in picture 64) and the defective loading gauge. Both ends should be raised to avoid trimming the driver's eyebrows. (H.C.Casserley)

66. The west elevation emphasises the elegant symmetry of the simple design, a good starting point for railway modellers. There were 1199 tickets sold in 1938, generating a revenue of £82. (R.M.Casserley)

67. Few would believe that this was an operational railway only 10 months earlier. However, the sign board was still standing 17 years after the last passenger had needed to know their whereabouts. (R.M.Casserley)

BACTON

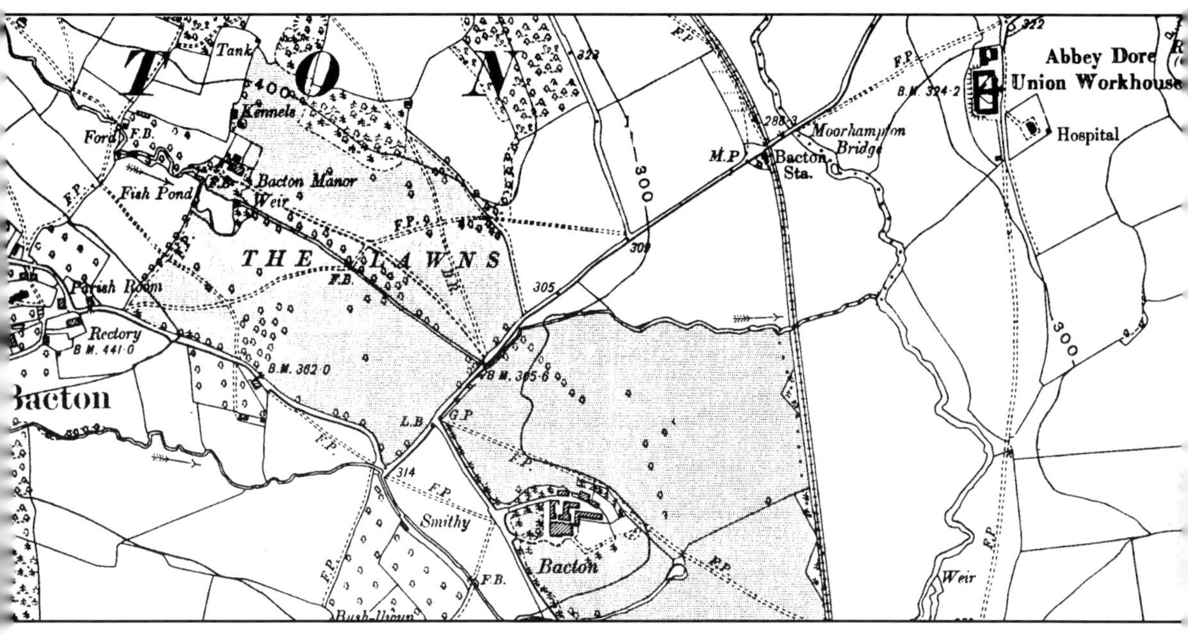

XVII. This station was added by the GWR optimistically, although the GVR listed "Bacton Road" as a request stop. A weighbridge was provided in 1903. There were 148 souls here in 1901, the figure halving in the next 60 years.

68. This snowy view is towards Hay in the 1930s. Advertising here would have been of limited value. The lantern door has been left hanging open. (Lens of Sutton coll.)

69. A photograph from 21st June 1951 shows the fireman of 1400 class 0-4-2T no. 5818 rejoining the footplate, as the guard would open the gates to road traffic. Beyond them is a goods loop; the end of a van therein is evident. The yard was used for the assembly of flat-pack Allis-Chalmers tractors imported from the USA in 1941. (SLS coll.)

PONTRILAS, DORSTONE, and HAY.—Golden Valley.
Sec., David S. Derry. Man., J. W. Marshall. All 1 & 3 class.

Frm London, p.32.	mrn	gov	mrn	mrn	aft	aft
Pontrilas.....dep	7 15	8 45	10 5	1150	2 0	4 50
Abbeydore	7 21	8 50	1011	1156	2 10	4 56
Vowchurch	7 32	9 0	1021	12 5	2 22	5 7
Peterchurch......	7 37	9 5	1026	1210	2 30	5 13
Dorstone	7 48	9 16	1037	1221	2 45	5 24
Westbrook........	Weds only.	9 27	11 0	1231	3 56	6 15
Clifford...........		9 37	11 9	1240	4 10	6 24
Hay 270......arr		9 45	1115	1247	4 17	6 30

Down.	mrn	gov	mrn	mrn	aft	aft	
Hay........dep	Weds only.	8 45	1020	1150	3 0	5 40	....
Clifford........		8 55	1030	12 0	3 10	5 50	....
Westbrook.....		9 5	1040	1210	3 20	5 59	....
Dorstone......	7 55	9 15	1050	1220	3 30	6 5	....
Peterchurch ...	8 5	9 25	11 7	1231	3 47	6 17	....
Vowchurch	8 10	9 30	1112	1236	3 55	6 22	....
Abbeydore. .[32	8 21	9 40	1123	1245	4 10	6 33	....
Pontrilas 33,ar	8 27	9 45	1129	1251	4 19	6 40	....

February 1890

PONTRILAS, DORSTONE, and HAY—(**Third class only**).

Miles	**Down.**	**Week Days only.**						
		mrn						
	Pontrilas..........dep.	8 40	..	..	..	..	..	..
2¼	Abbeydore..................	8 45	..	..	..	..	..	..
3¾	Bacton......................	8 48	..	..	..	..	..	..
6¼	Vowchurch..................	8 58	..	..	..	..	..	..
7¾	Peterchurch................	9 5	..	..	..	..	..	..
10¼	Dorstone....................	9 19	..	..	..	..	..	..
13¼	Westbrook	9 29	..	..	..	..	..	..
14¼	Greens Siding............	9 32	..	..	..	..	..	..
16¼	Clifford	9 40	..	..	..	..	..	..
18¼	**Hay 699**...........arr.	9 53	..	..	..	..	..	..

Miles	**Up.**	**Week Days only.**							
		mrn							
	Hay..................dep.	1025	..	..	..	..	..	..	..
2¼	Clifford	1032	..	..	..	..	..	..	..
4½	Greens Siding............	1038	..	..	..	..	..	..	..
5¼	Westbrook..................	1042	..	..	..	..	..	..	..
8¼	Dorstone....................	1050	..	..	..	..	..	..	..
11	Peterchurch................	11 2	..	..	..	..	..	..	..
12¾	Vowchurch	1114	..	..	..	..	..	..	..
15¼	Bacton.......................	1128	..	..	..	..	..	..	..
16¼	Abbeydore..................	1135	..	..	..	..	..	..	..
18½	**Pontrilas 122,125**..arr.	1143	..	..	..	..	..	..	..

November 194

VOWCHURCH

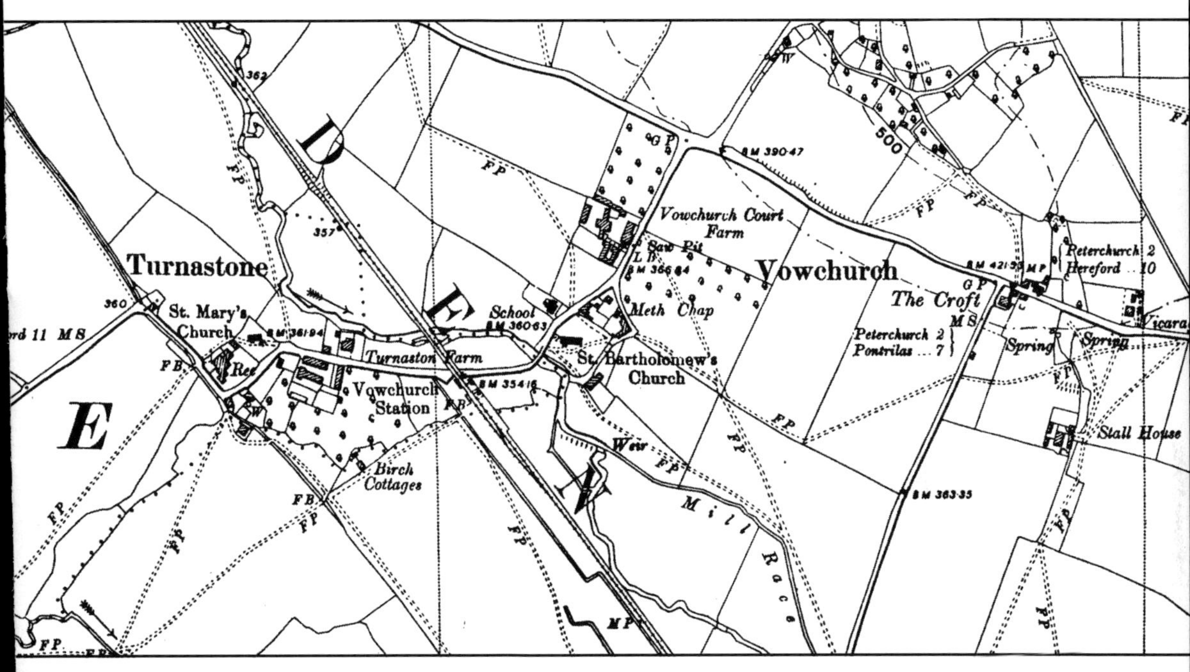

XVIII. The station was close to the community, which comprised only 280 souls in 1901 and it dropped subsequently.

70. A staff of one was listed throughout the GWR years and the photographer has interrupted the gardening in this postcard view. (Lens of Sutton coll.)

71. The general managers office was here in the first years of the GVR. It may be the building in the distance. Near it is a crane used for loading timber, a traffic which ceased in 1952. (R.M.Casserley coll.)

XIX. The 1904 survey reveals the proximity of the watercourses.

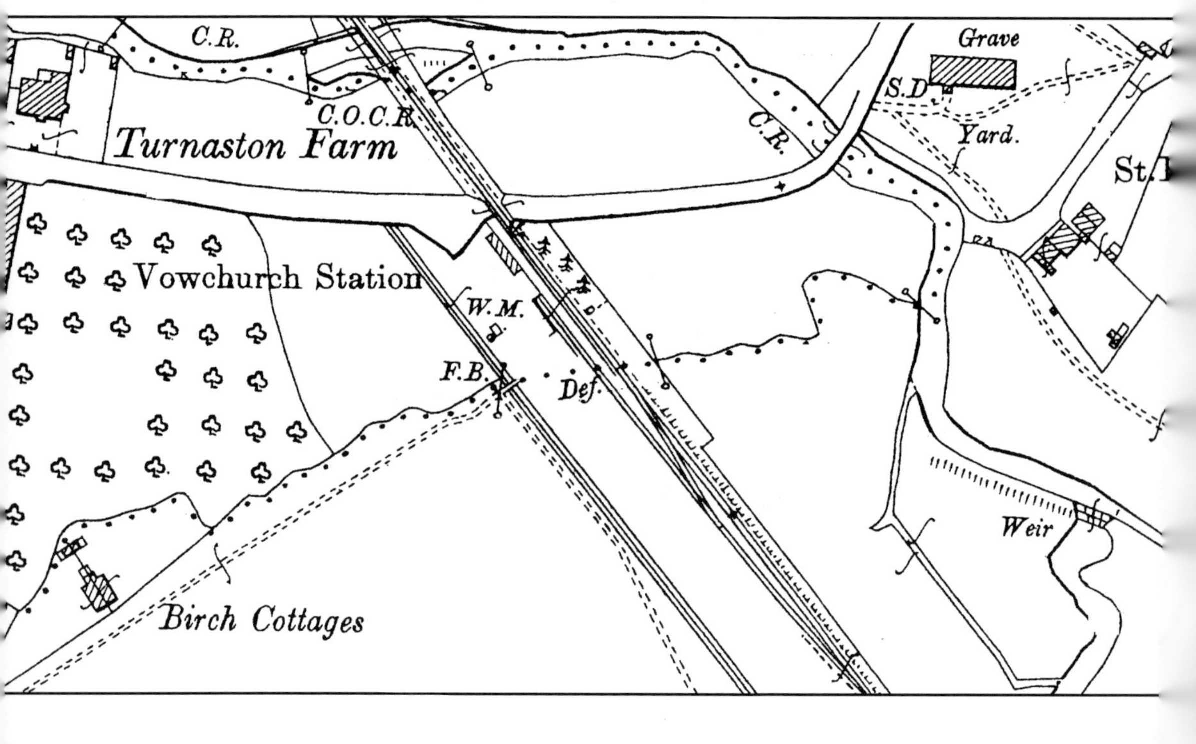

72. The title could be "Two Pints Please and Mind My Bike". The fact is that this picture was taken a short while after no. 63, as the train returns downhill. All traffic ceased on 2nd February 1953. (SLS coll.)

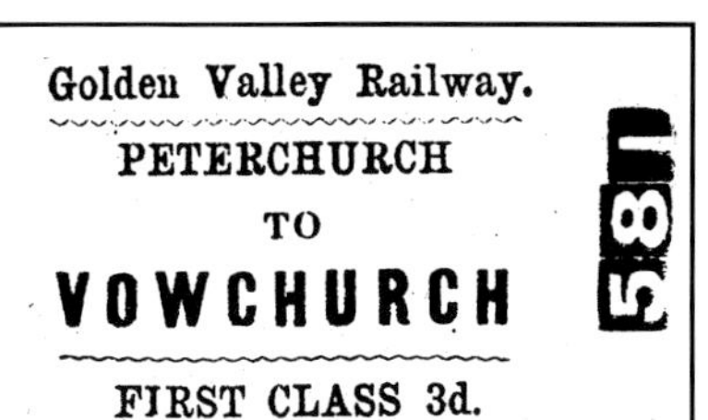

Golden Valley Railway.
PETERCHURCH
TO
VOWCHURCH
FIRST CLASS 3d.

Vowchurch	**1903**	**1913**	**1923**	**1932**
Passenger tickets issued	4390	3644	3373	785
Season tickets issued	*	*	-	9
Parcels forwarded	711	842	910	781
General goods forwarded (tons)	612	1073	851	1424
Coal and coke received (tons)	663	431	471	289
Other minerals received (tons)	425	785	480	627
General goods received (tons)	715	589	296	156
Trucks of livestock handled	1	1	3	12

(* not available.)

PETERCHURCH

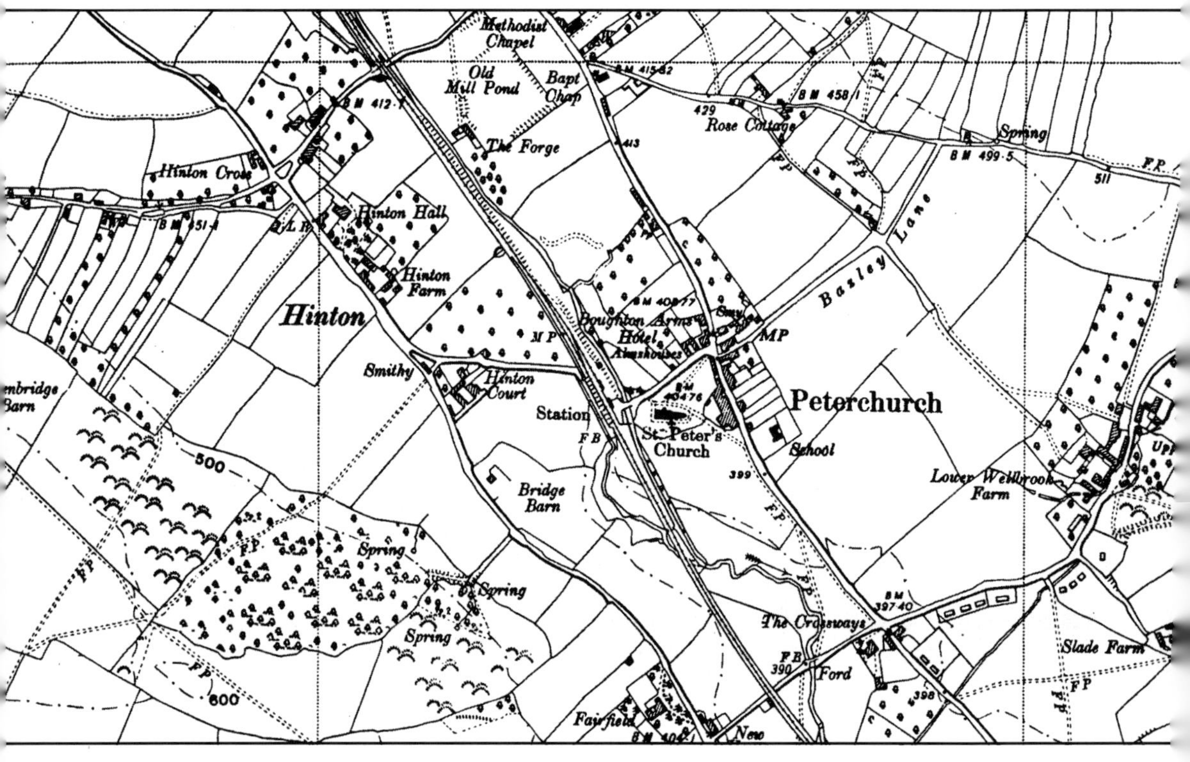

XX. The 1952 survey includes extensive signs of habitation, but the population was under 600 during the life of the line.

73. This photograph is annotated 1887 and four-wheeled carriages are included, the braked vehicle having a birdcage lookout. The wagon is from a Pontypool colliery. The church bells rang out when the railway opened and again when it reopened. (P.Q.Treloar coll.)

74. This view has been dated as 1909; the goods shed was added in 1903. The GWR provided three men from that year until at least 1938. Much wool was despatched by rail from here. (Lens of Sutton coll.)

XXI. The 1904 extract reveals the circuitous route of the lane round the station.

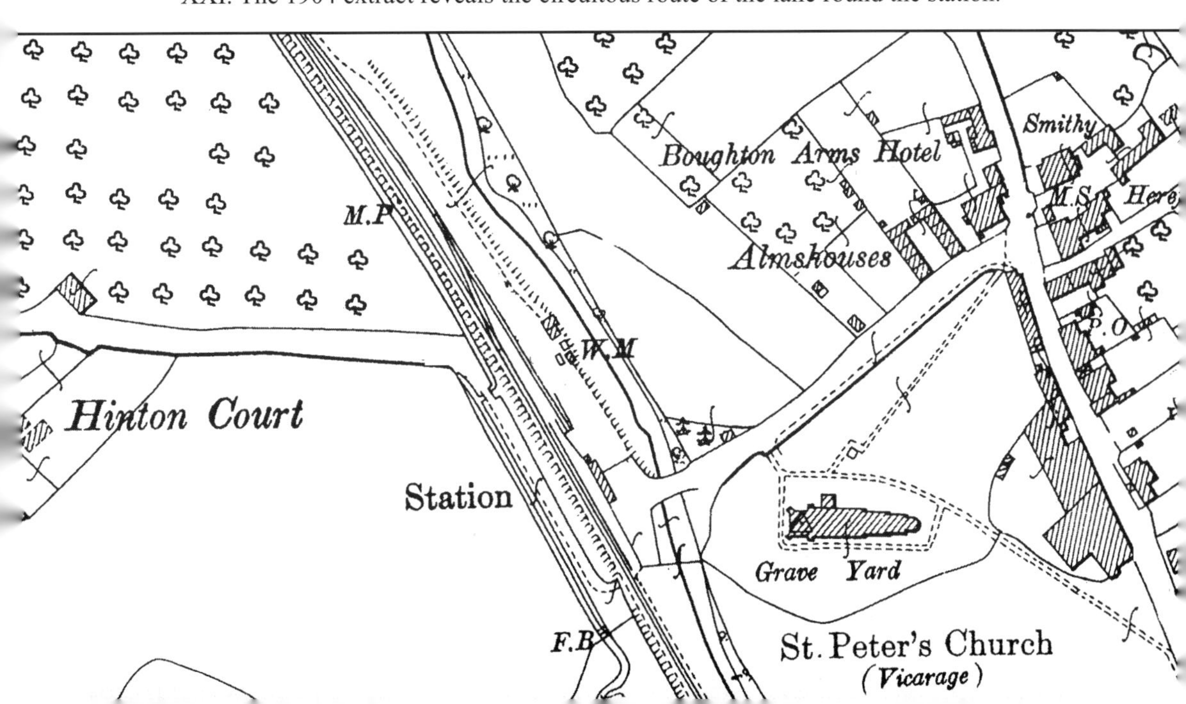

75. A 517 class 0-4-2T runs in over the level crossing and approaches a rare commodity in our pictures: passengers. The river ran immediately behind the building and passengers passed over a bridge to reach the village. (Lens of Sutton coll.)

Peterchurch	**1903**	**1913**	**1923**	**1933**
Passenger tickets issued	5532	4392	3586	774
Season tickets issued	*	*	12	-
Parcels forwarded	1916	4083	2589	1527
General goods forwarded (tons)	267	539	498	133
Coal and coke received (tons)	395	310	318	119
Other minerals received (tons)	245	754	511	131
General goods received (tons)	1441	792	781	782
Trucks of livestock handled	6	12	143	32

(* not available.)

76. The cattle dock is in the distance; there was a livestock market nearby until 1956. The goods loop starts near the dock. All traffic ceased on 2nd February 1953. (R.M.Casserley coll.)

77. Regardless of the 1958 evidence, the best way to travel in this world is the railway and the best way to the next is the church. (H.C.Casserley)

DORSTONE

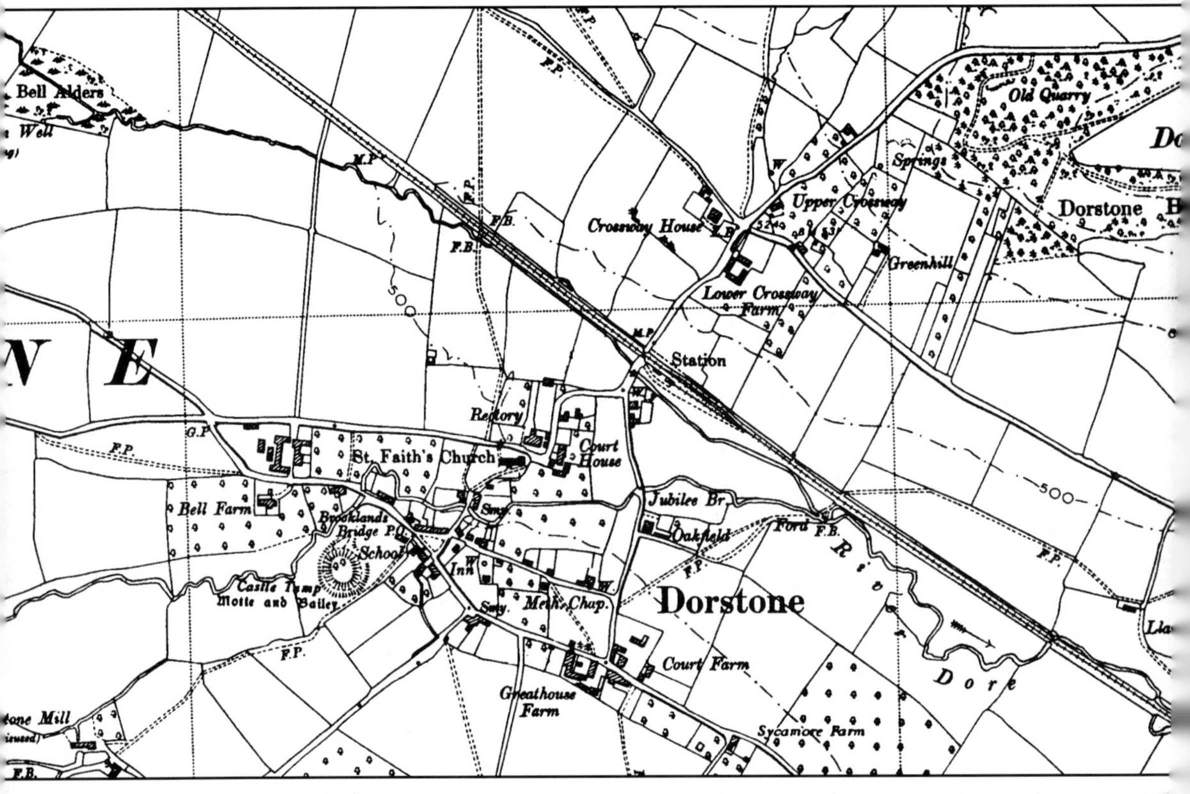

XXII. The River Dore is of a minor nature in this vicinity and some springs are evident on this 1952 map. The summit of the line is reached between here and Westbrook, part of the climb being at 1 in 75.

78. There is no record of more than one man being employed here. He seems to have specialised in rockeries. The parcels shed was completed in 1881. (Postcard)

79. No. 5818 was recorded on 30th August 1941. It is an 0-4-2T of the 1400 class, based at Pontypool Road. There were 398 inhabitants in 1901 and only 301 in 1961. (F.K.Davies/R.M.Casserley coll.)

XXIII. The 1904 survey shows a shelter on the second platform.

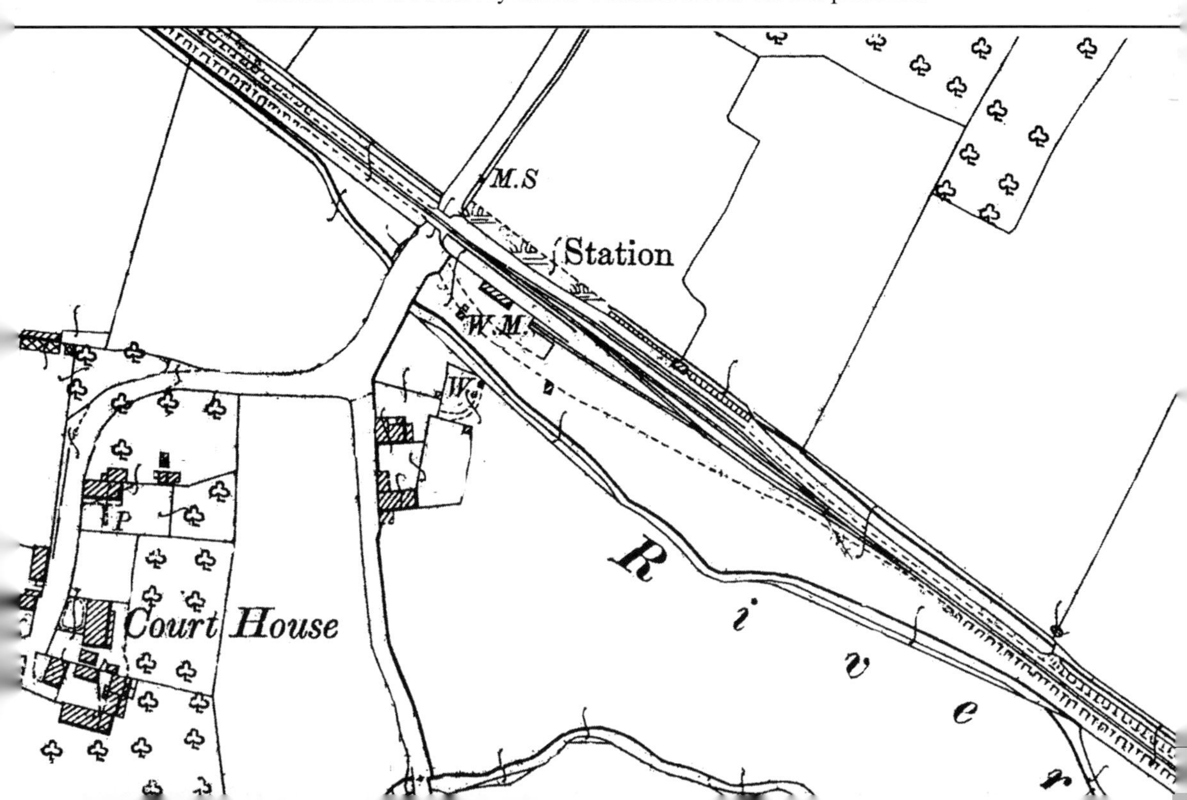

80. The original timber buildings were supplied by the Gloucester Carriage & Wagon Company for all the stations, except Bacton. This 1948 panorama includes the second platform; this was the only GVR station to have one and it was only used briefly. (R.G.Nelson/T.Walsh coll.)

5185

Gt. Western Ry. Gt. Western Ry.
HAY HAY
TO
CLIFFORD
2½d. THIRD CLASS 2½d.
Issued subject to the conditions & regulations set out in the Company's Time Tables, Bills & Notices
Clifford Clifford

5185

Dorstone	1903	1913	1923	1933
Passenger tickets issued	5072	4513	3650	590
Season tickets issued	*	*	-	1
Parcels forwarded	1554	2125	987	1894
General goods forwarded (tons)	129	280	1102	477
Coal and coke received (tons)	241	197	120	55
Other minerals received (tons)	176	387	428	186
General goods received (tons)	267	401	317	79
Trucks of livestock handled	3	43	31	21

(* not available.)

81. A 1950 record includes the ends of both loops. Goods traffic would continue until 2nd February 1953. This had been the end of the line since 1949. (R.M.Casserley coll.)

82. The little used platform is seen in 1956. Back in 1950-52, there had been an excursion train to Porthcawl each August, the train usually comprising five coaches. (SLS coll.)

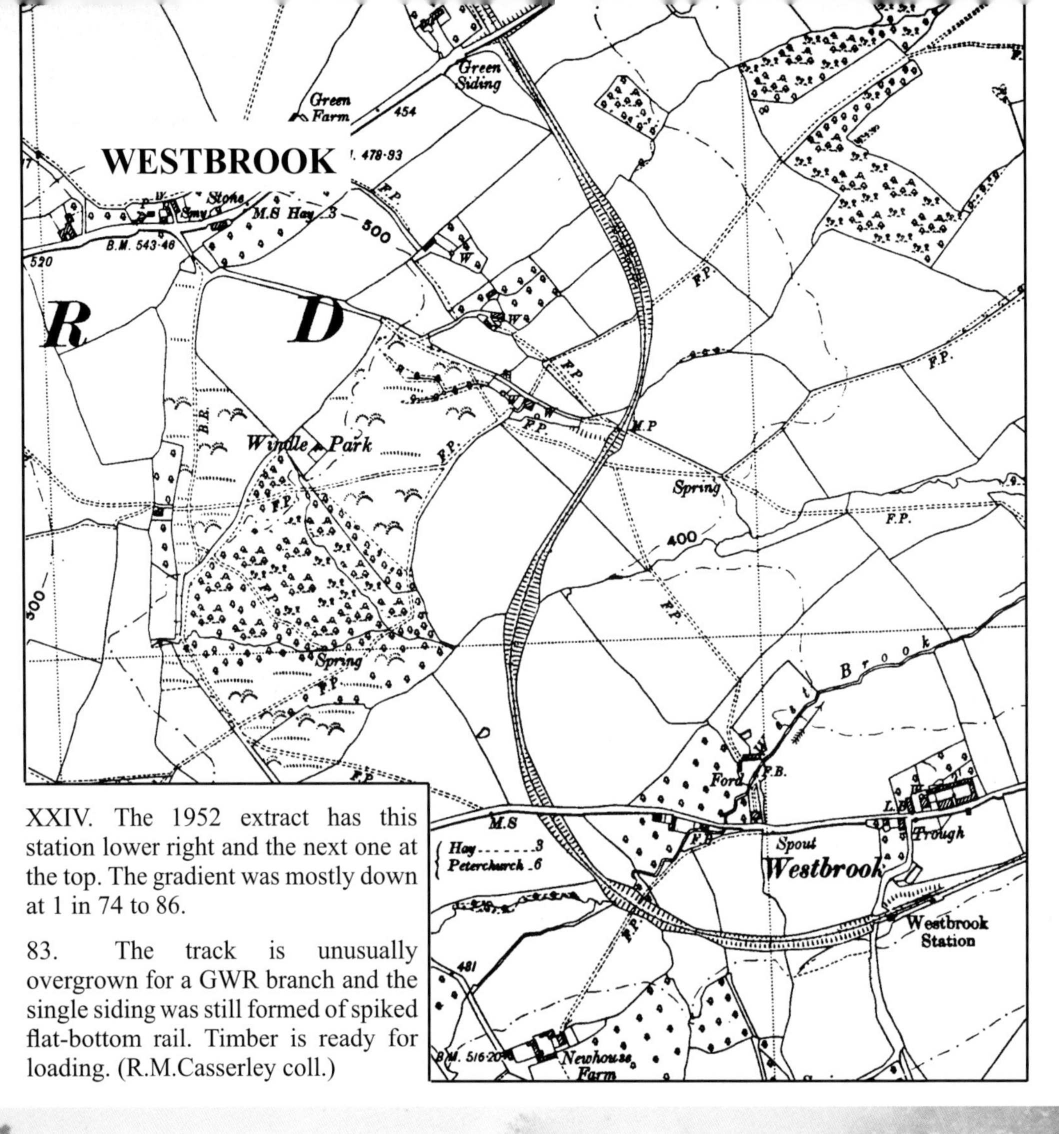

XXIV. The 1952 extract has this station lower right and the next one at the top. The gradient was mostly down at 1 in 74 to 86.

83. The track is unusually overgrown for a GWR branch and the single siding was still formed of spiked flat-bottom rail. Timber is ready for loading. (R.M.Casserley coll.)

84. The stone-built structure was still standing in July 1958. One man was provided until the mid-1920s and mostly three in the 1930s. (R.M.Casserley)

XXV. The 1904 edition.

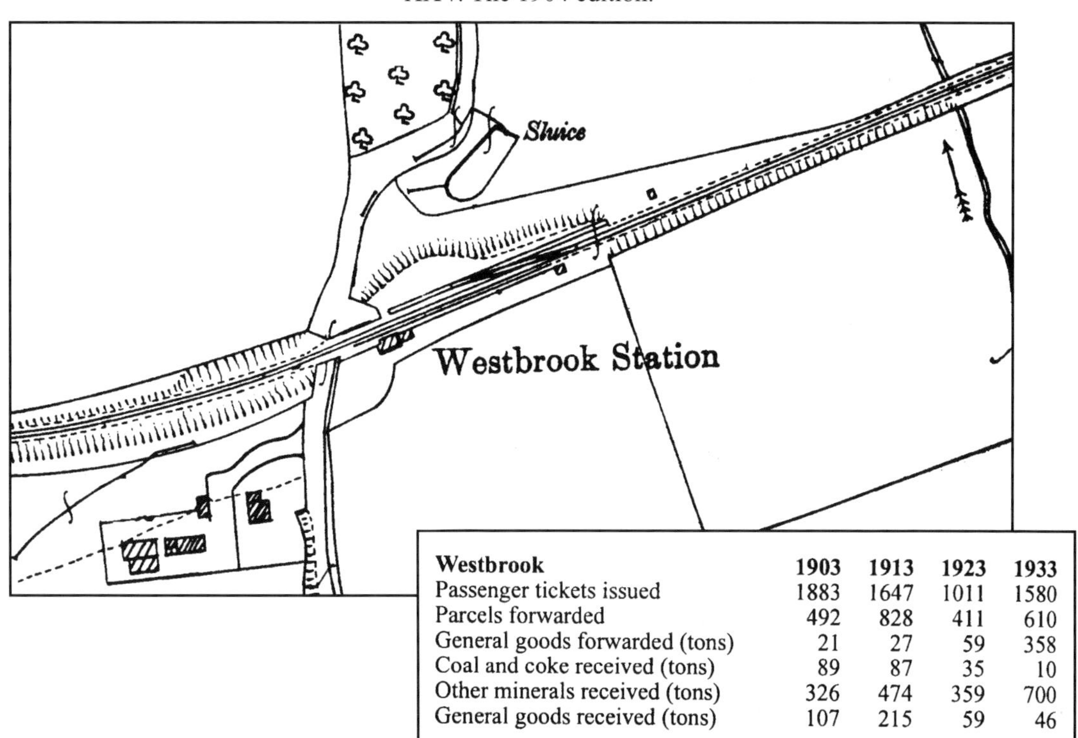

Westbrook	1903	1913	1923	1933
Passenger tickets issued	1883	1647	1011	1580
Parcels forwarded	492	828	411	610
General goods forwarded (tons)	21	27	59	358
Coal and coke received (tons)	89	87	35	10
Other minerals received (tons)	326	474	359	700
General goods received (tons)	107	215	59	46

GREENS SIDING

85. The siding was south of the bridge and the platform north of it. Both were provided by the GWR in 1903. One man was employed here until 1924. Dew Siding was the name employed by the GVR for a facility in this vicinity. (LGRP)

86. The site of the goods yard and its approach road were recorded in April 1961. The siding was formed into a loop in 1904 and reported as lifted in 1924. However, it was still showing in some lists at the end, in 1949. (J.Langford)

CLIFFORD

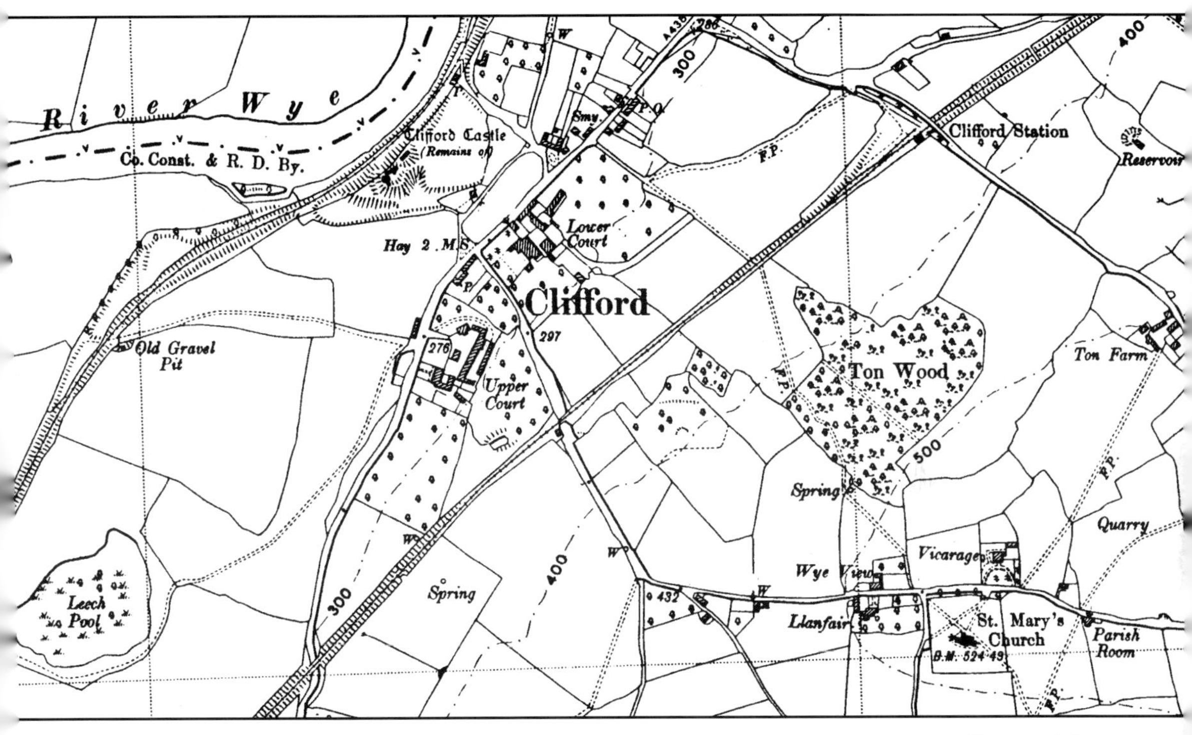

XXVI. The 1945 survey has the line from Hereford top centre and our route from Pontrilas top right. The former is more than 100ft below the latter. The population was 730 in 1901 and 586 in 1961.

87. Stone-built like the second batch of GVR stations elsewhere, this one was unusual in having a water tank. This is explained by the presence of an engine shed here until 1897; it had been in the right foreground. Two men were provided in the early years of the GWR. (LGRP)

88. A 1945 panorama includes the 1903 cattle pen. The single siding had been converted to a loop in 1888, but most of the track was relaid in 1900. It was all lifted in 1949. (S.H.P.Higgins)

XXVII. The 1903 survey reveals the old route of the road.

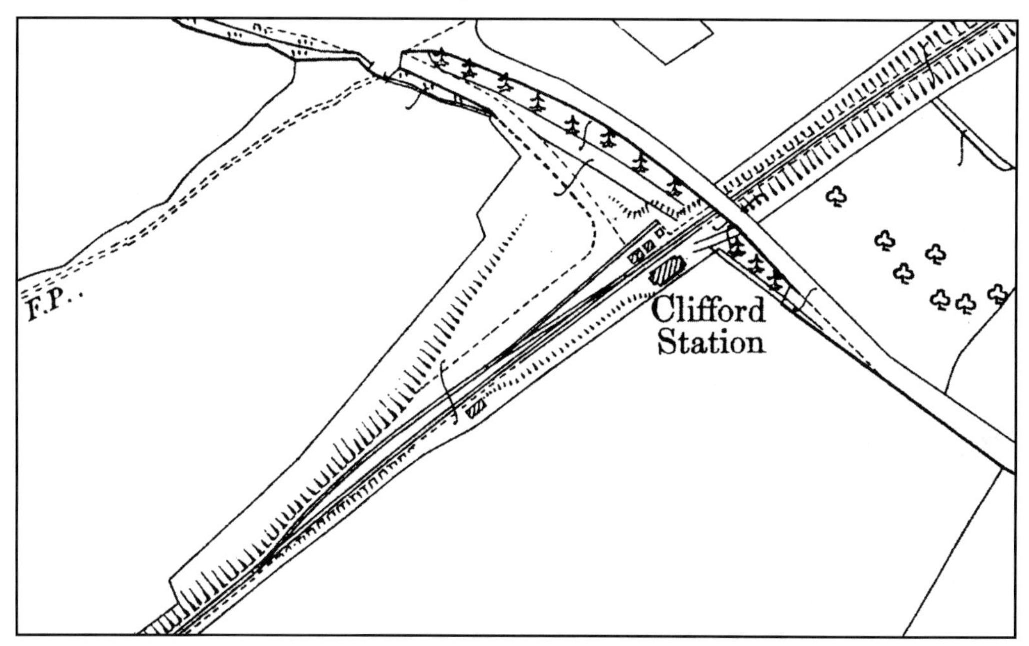

HAY-ON-WYE

89. This southward view is from about 1900 and the prolific enamel signs are on painted palings. The MR later standardised on inclined creosoted fencing. (R.S.Carpenter coll.)

90. A late 19th century photograph features the footbridge from which many other pictures were taken. The shadow of Station Box is in the left foreground; the box was in use until 1st January 1963. (R.S.Carpenter coll.)

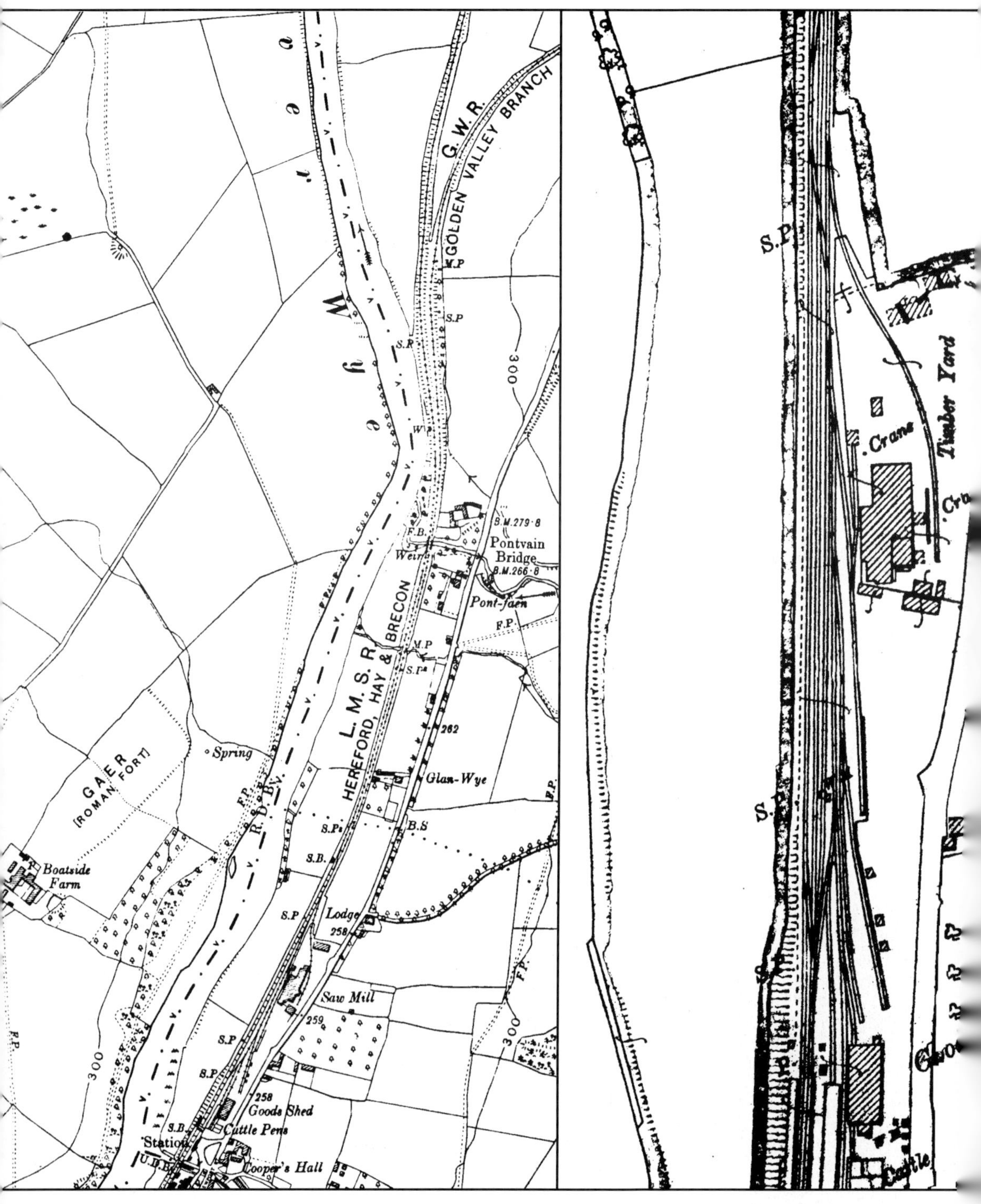

XXVIII. The 1945 survey has the line from Hereford at the top and indicates the positions of both signal boxes with S.B.

XXIX. The 1904 edition gives the details of the goods yard and also the timber yard, the line to which passes through a gateway. The firm was listed as R.Williams & Sons in 1938.

91. An Edwardian postcard shows the benefit of the then new high speed cameras and the complexity of carriage gas light plumbing. The leading coach would run through to Swansea. (Lens of Sutton coll.)

92. Another train with a clerestory through coach has taken water, the storage tank being on the left. The town is in the left background. (Lens of Sutton coll.)

93. A 1932 northward view has Junction Box in the distance and, on the right an early horse box, plus part of a cattle wagon. The box had 28 levers. (Mowat coll./Brunel University)

94. The bridge in the background carries the road to Clyro, the B4351 since numbering started in 1919. The photograph is from 1933 and includes the rodding tunnel. (R.M.Casserley coll.)

95. A record from 4th May 1948 includes the up platform waiting shelter and water column. Up departures at this time were at 7.39, 11.19am and 2.7, 6.49pm. (R.G.Nelson/T.Walsh coll.)

96. Displaying the early BR lettering, class 3F no. 52525 waits by the goods shed on 9th September 1949. The shed contained a 30cwt crane. The lion and monocycle logo was soon to be introduced. (H.C.Casserley)

97. Three despondent passengers are seen on the same day. Hay Urban District Council added "on Wye" to the name of the town in 1947, but BR did not adopt it until 13th June 1955. The goods shed and yard was later used for storage by Brecon & Radnor Farmers. (H.C.Casserley)

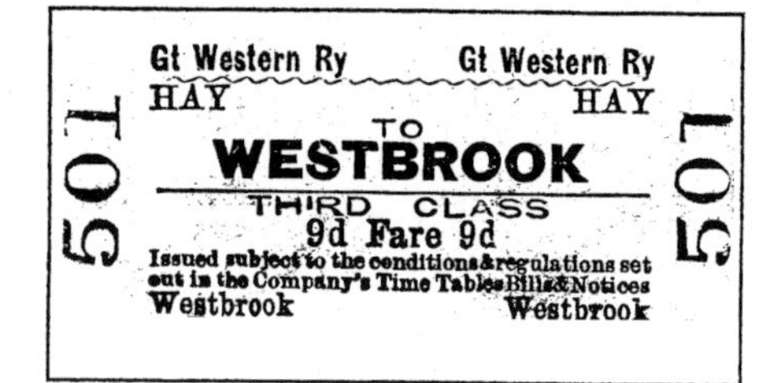
501
Gt Western Ry Gt Western Ry
HAY HAY
TO
WESTBROOK
THIRD CLASS
9d Fare 9d
Issued subject to the conditions®ulations set out in the Company's Time TablesBills&Notices
Westbrook Westbrook
501

6344
Gt Western Ry. Gt. Western Ry
HAY HAY
TO
GREEN'S SIDING
THIRD CLASS
7½d Fare 7½d
Issued subject to the conditions®ulations set out in the Company's Time Tables,Bills&Notices
Green's Siding Green's Siding
6344

98. This is the 4.5pm from Hereford on 8th May 1953. Typical of the era was no. 43491, an ex-MR 0-6-0 classified 3F and of a type introduced in 1885. (T.J.Edgington)

99. The signalman waits to exchange tablets with the driver of ex-GWR 0-6-0 no. 2275 on 13th September 1956. It is working the 4.15pm from Brecon, while no. 2287 is on the 4.5 from Hereford. Station Box had 16 levers. (R.M.Casserley)

100. This northward panorama from 1958 was shot from the then boundary between England and Wales. After more reorganisation, the town has returned there again, being now in Powys. (R.M.Casserley)

101. The youngest locomotives to frequent the route were the 2F 2-6-0s introduced by the LMS in 1946. One such is no. 46507, which was heading a train for Hereford on 10th August 1960. A string of cattle wagons is in the yard. (Millbrook House)

102. Taking water on 28th May 1961 is ex-GWR 0-6-0PT no. 9644 at the head of a troop special. The Army had training grounds on the moors beyond Brecon. (P.Hay)

103. A few minutes later and it becomes apparent that there are two Pannier tanks and that the train is very long. National Service was still in force, but for men only. (P.Hay)

104. The approach was photographed in 1961, the year in which the census returned 1320 inhabitants. Economy was still the desire of most people, the Bond three-wheeler exemplifying this. (Lens of Sutton coll.)

105. A goods train bound for Brecon approaches the water column sometime in 1962. No. 78004 was one of the BR 2-6-0s. Passenger services ceased here at the end of that year. The goods facility was retained as a non-rail connected depot until 28th September 1964. (M.J.Stretton coll.)

106. Class 2F no. 46510 is central in this view across the international boundary on 1st October 1962. All was swept away to make space for a superstore. The town was to gain fame as a book centre; there were 39 such shops in the area in 2006. (G.Adams/M.J.Stretton coll.)

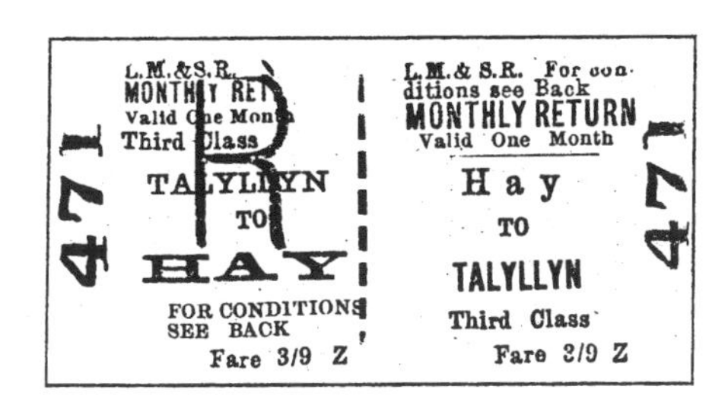

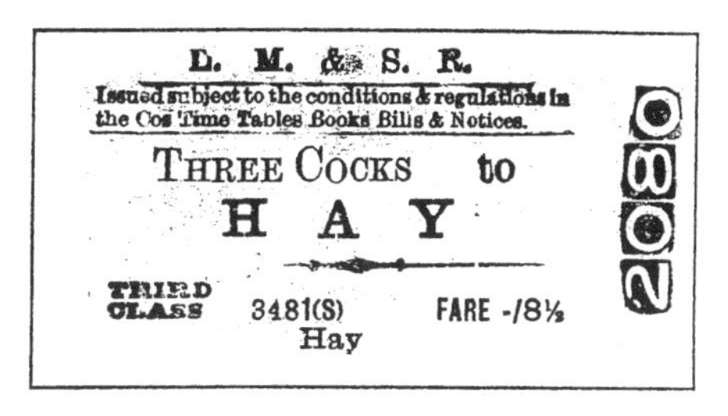

GLASBURY-ON-WYE

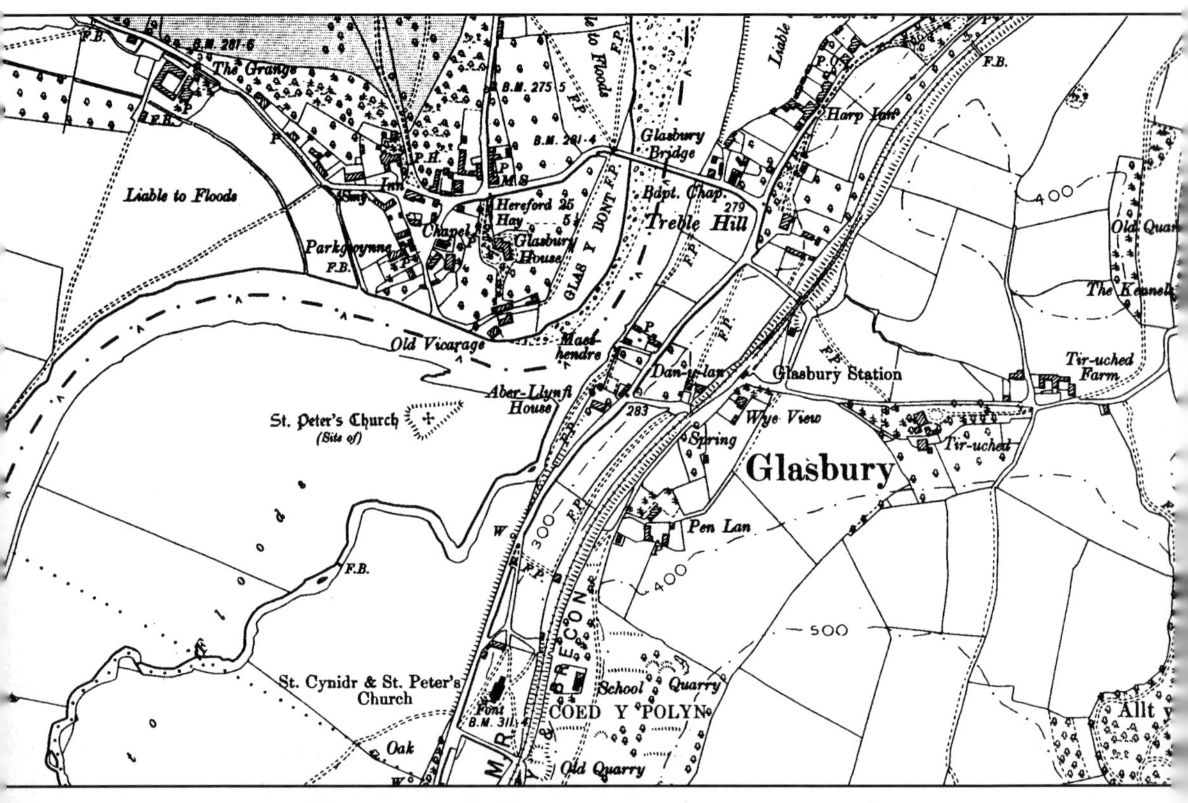

XXX. The 1904 edition shows that most of the village was north of the river and thus in Radnorshire. The suffix was added to the station name in 1894.

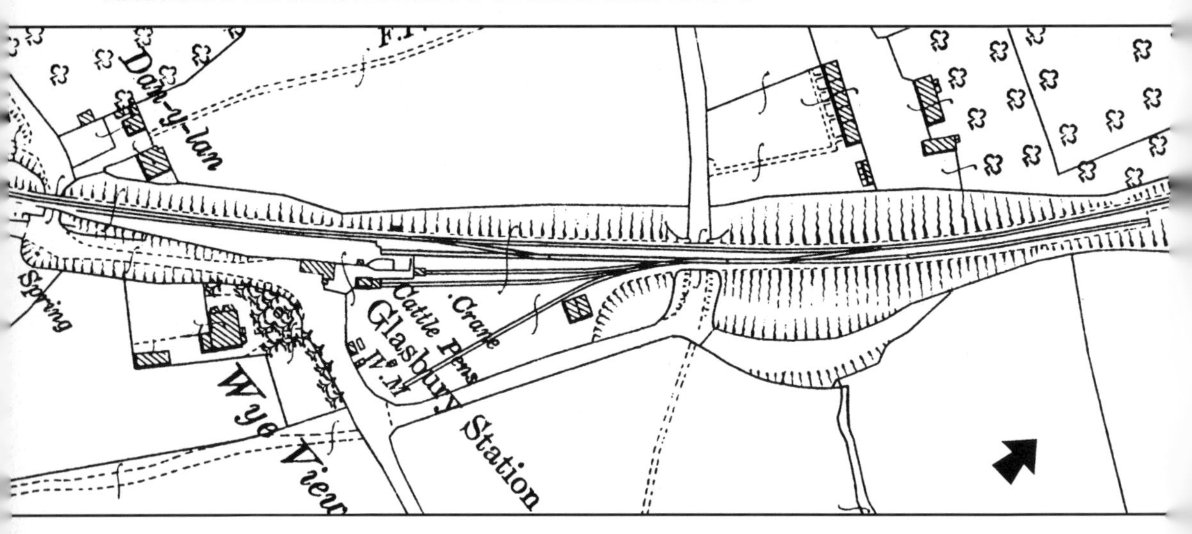

107. The end of the shorter of the two sidings was photographed on 6th July 1958, along with the well maintained lanterns. The population dropped from 460 in 1901 to 363 in 1961. (R.M.Casserley)

108. The floral display is seen again on the same day, along with evidence of platform lengthening. The building was probably erected remote from the platform edge so that it was not on made-up ground. The track was on a shelf on the steep side of the valley. (H.C.Casserley)

109. Goods and passenger traffic ceased here at the end of 1962, the year in which this photograph was taken. No. 46516 was a sister to those seen in pictures 101 and 106. (Millbrook House)

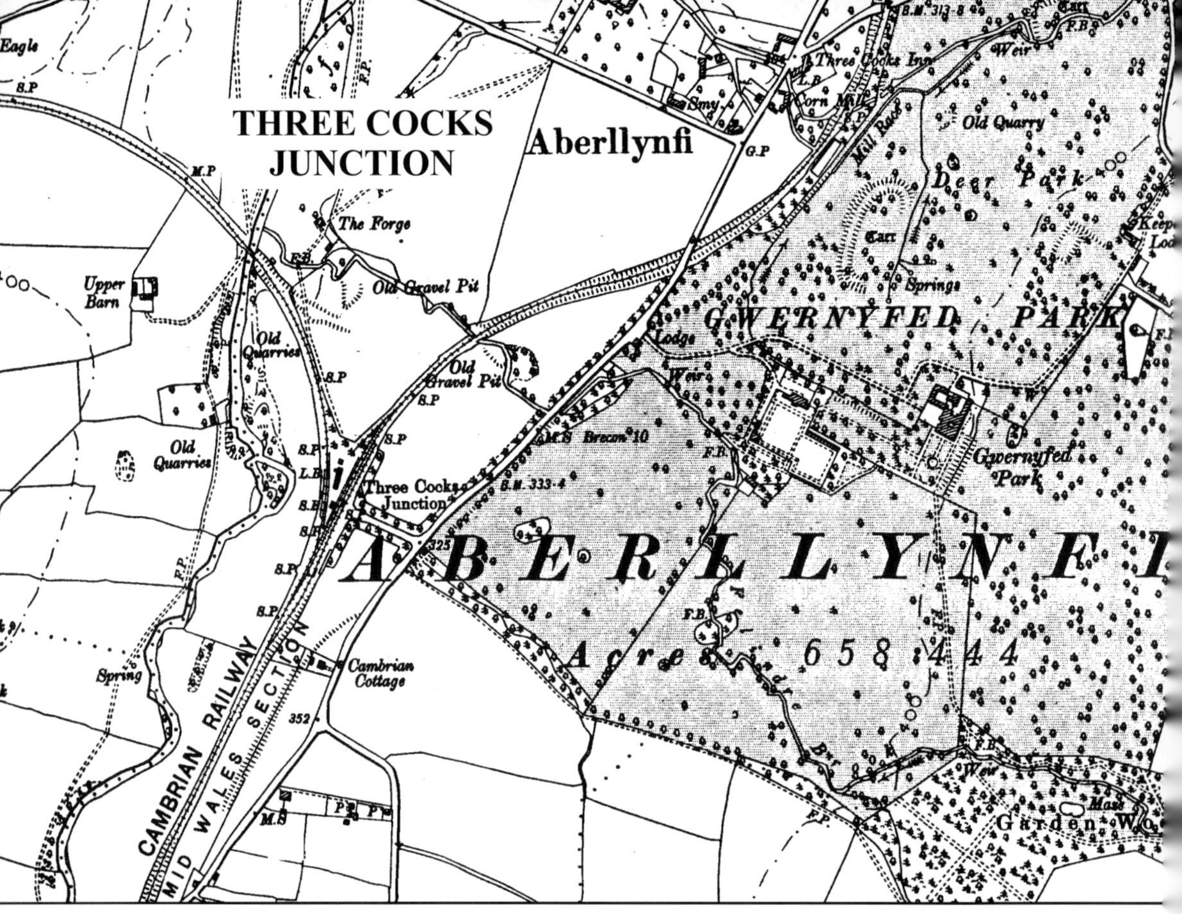

XXXI. The inn after which the station was named is top right on this 1905 map. The railway promoters probably preferred this name to the Welsh one for the village. It had only 168 residents when the line closed.

110. The postcard producer was helpful to his customers (and us), but did not go as far as noting that all passengers changing trains here had to cross the tracks on the level, an advantage with luggage. (P.Q.Treloar coll.)

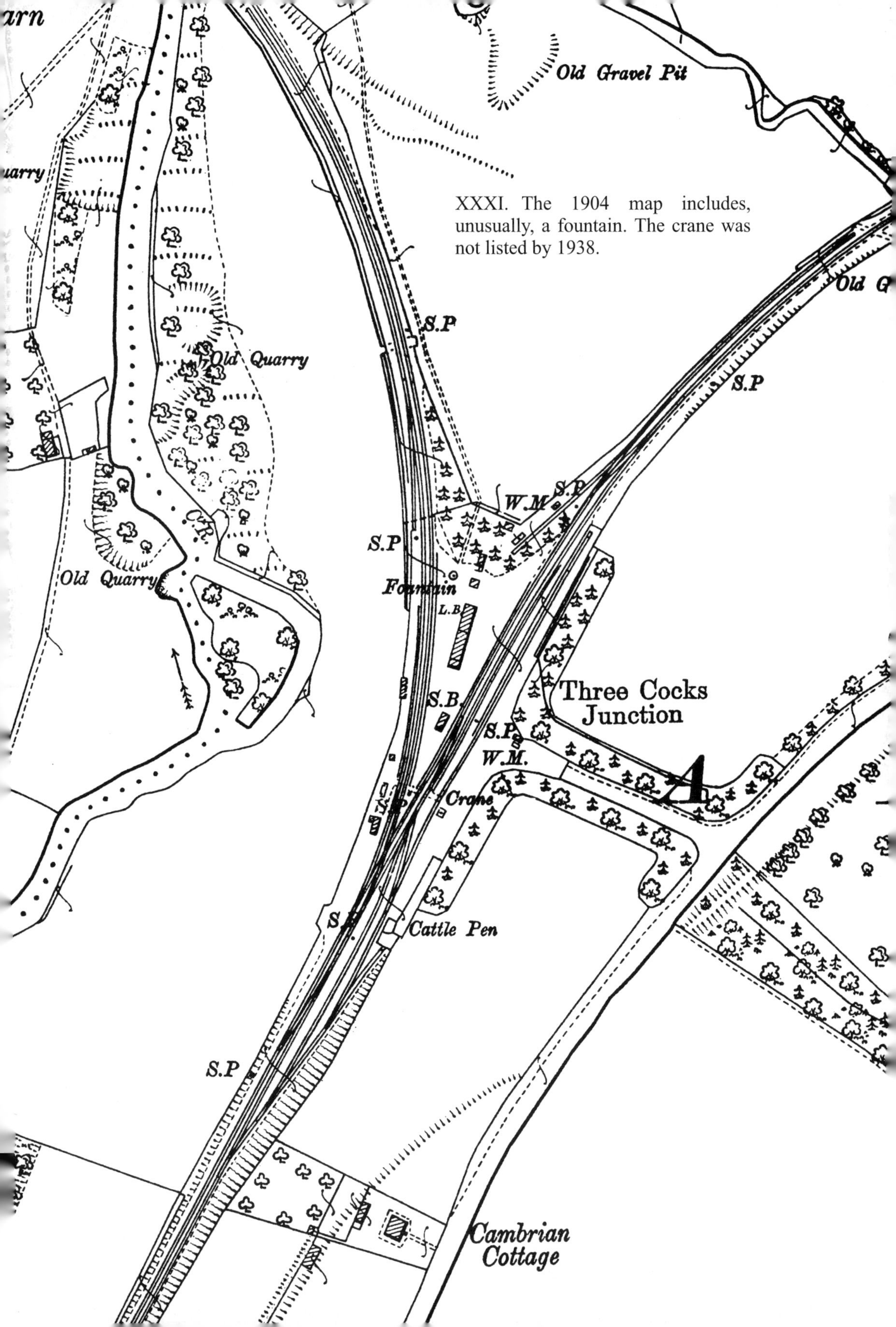

XXXI. The 1904 map includes, unusually, a fountain. The crane was not listed by 1938.

111. The 1.10pm Brecon to Hereford was hauled by class 3F 0-6-0 no. 43600 on 9th September 1949. The locomotive was based at Pontypool Road, although the shed plate suggests Bletchley. (H.C.Casserley)

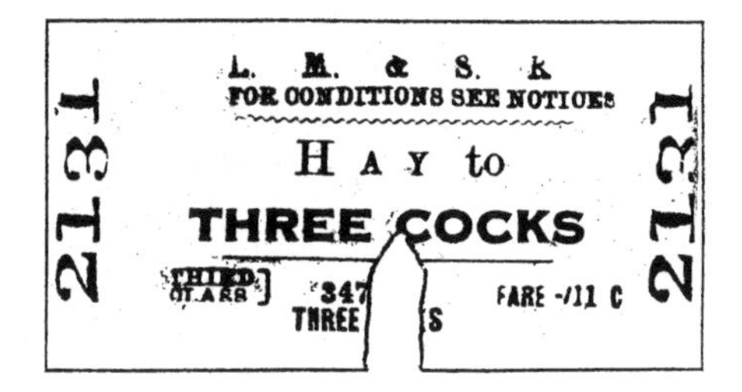

112. Although the loco is in shadow, this photograph is useful in that it is the only one to show the entrance and that the main gates were supplemented by a "kissing gate", an unusual feature when no cattle were involved. (R.Holmes)

113. On the right is the western end of the MR from Hereford, the curved lines having been the property of the Cambrian Railways. This and the next picture were taken on 13th September 1956. (R.M.Casserley)

114. Taken against the light, this photograph includes the sign offering the opportunity to change for Builth Wells, Llandrindod Wells, Llanidloes and the Cambrian Coast. The sidings seem full. (R.M.Casserley)

115. Looking like a dwelling, this building was a memorable feature of the junction and included a licensed refreshment room. The platforms were very low and so a flight of two portable steps were provided, complete with handrails and two small trolley wheels. It is next to the sack truck. (D.Lawrence)

116. No. 46516 (right) has arrived with a train from Hereford on 23rd August 1961. On the left is no. 46505 with a Builth Road (Low Level) to Brecon service. Some passengers had to walk across a siding as well as the running lines. (E.Wilmshurst)

117. From left to right (with loco numbers) are the 1.20pm Brecon to Moat Lane Junction (46501), the 12.30 Builth Road to Brecon (46523) and the 2.15 Three Cocks Junction to Hereford (46513). The date is 14th April 1962 and the sidings are shown in full. (J.Langford)

118. A delightful panorama from earlier the same day shows no. 46523 ready to leave tender first for Builth Road at 11.15. It had connected with the 10.25 from Brecon. (J.Langford)

119. The same locomotive had earlier worked the 9.10am from Builth Road that day and it is seen after terminating at 10.4. The 10.12 to Brecon was due from Hereford at 10.8. The signal box had 40 levers and was not required after 1962. (J.Langford)

120. The site became an industrial estate, but we can live with the memory of this rural junction, by imprinting in the mind this fine record of one of the best of the light engines to last to the end of the BR steam era. (G.Adams/M.J.Stretton coll.)

2nd · SINGLE SINGLE · 2nd
3730 3730
Three Cocks to
Three Cocks Three Cocks
Glasbury on Wye Glasbury on Wye
GLASBURY ON WYE
(W) 4d. FARE 4d. (W)
For conditions see over For conditions see over

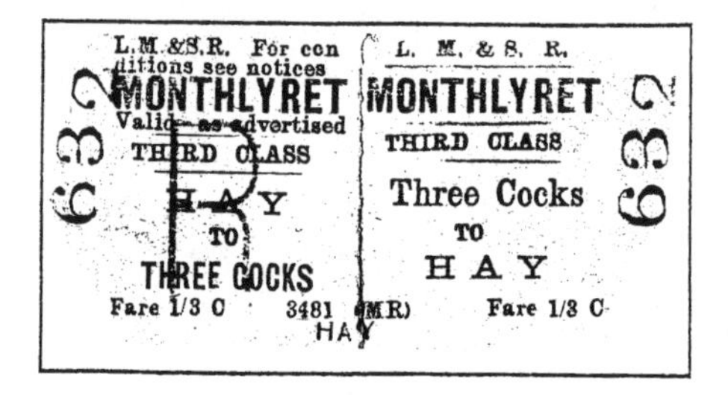

THREE COCKS Jn SIGNAL BOX
46510

EVOLVING THE ULTIMATE RAIL ENCYCLOPEDIA

Easebourne Lane, Midhurst, West Sussex.
GU29 9AZ Tel:01730 813169
www.middletonpress.co.uk email:info@middletonpress.co.uk

A-0 906520 B-1 873793 C-1 901706 D-1 904474

OOP Out of print at time of printing - Please check availability BROCHURE AVAILABLE SHOWING NEW TITLES

A
Abergavenny to Merthyr C 91 5
Abertillery and Ebbw Vale Lines D 84 5
Aldgate & Stepney Tramways B 70 7
Allhallows - Branch Line to A 62 2
Alton - Branch Lines to A 11 8
Andover to Southampton A 82 7
Ascot - Branch Lines around A 64 9
Ashburton - Branch Line to B 95 2
Ashford - Steam to Eurostar B 67 7
Ashford to Dover A 48 7
Austrian Narrow Gauge D 04 7
Avonmouth - BL around D 42 X
Aylesbury to Rugby D 91 8
B
Baker Street to Uxbridge D 90 X
Banbury to Birmingham D 27 6
Barking to Southend C 80 X
Barnet & Finchley Tramways B 93 6
Barry - Branch Lines around D 50 0
Basingstoke to Salisbury A 89 4
Bath Green Park to Bristol C 36 2
Bath to Evercreech Junction A 60 6
Bath Tramways B 86 3
Battle over Portsmouth 1940 A 29 0
Battle over Sussex 1940 A 79 7
Bedford to Wellingborough D 31 4
Betwixt Petersfield & Midhurst A 94 0
Blitz over Sussex 1941-42 B 35 9
Bodmin - Branch Lines around B 83 9
Bognor at War 1939-45 B 59 6
Bombers over Sussex 1943-45 B 51 0
Bournemouth & Poole Trys B 47 2
Bournemouth to Evercreech Jn A 46 0
Bournemouth to Weymouth A 57 6
Bournemouth Trolleybuses C 10 9
Bradford Trolleybuses D 19 5
Branch Line to Hemel Hempstead D 88 8
Brecon to Neath D 43 8
Brecon to Newport D 16 0
Brickmaking in Sussex B 19 7
Brightons Tramways B 02 2 OOP
Brighton to Eastbourne A 16 9
Brighton to Worthing A 03 7
Brighton Trolleybuses D 34 9
Bristols Tramways B 57 X
Bristol to Taunton D 03 9
Bromley South to Rochester B 23 5
Bromsgrove to Birmingham D 87 X
Bromsgrove to Gloucester D 73 X
Brunel - A railtour of his achievements D 74 8
Bude - Branch Line to B 29 4
Burnham to Evercreech Jn A 68 1
Burton & Ashby Tramways C 51 6
C
Camberwell & West Norwood Tys B 22 7
Cambridge to Ely D 55 1
Canterbury - Branch Lines around B 58 8
Cardiff Trolleybuses D 64 0
Caterham & Tattenham Corner B 25 1
Changing Midhurst C 15 X
Chard and Yeovil - BLs around C 30 3
Charing Cross to Dartford A 75 4
Charing Cross to Orpington A 96 7
Cheddar - Branch Line to B 90 1
Cheltenham to Andover C 43 5
Cheltenham to Redditch D 81 0
Chesterfield Tramways D 37 3
Chesterfield Trolleybuses D 51 9
Chichester to Portsmouth A 14 2
Clapham & Streatham Trys B 97 9 OOP
Clapham Junction - 50 yrs C 06 0 OOP
Clapham Junction to Beckenham Jn B 36 7
Clevedon & Portishead - BLs to D 18 7
Collectors Trains, Trolleys & Trams D 29 2
Colonel Stephens D62 4
Cornwall Narrow Gauge D 56 X
Crawley to Littlehampton A 34 7
Cromer - Branch Lines around C 26 5
Croydons Tramways B 42 1
Croydons Trolleybuses B 73 1 OOP
Croydon to East Grinstead B 48 0
Crystal Palace (HL) & Catford Loop A 87 8
D
Darlington Trolleybuses D 33 0
Dartford to Sittingbourne B 34 0
Derby Tramways D 17 9
Derby Trolleybuses C 72 9
Derwent Valley - Branch Line to the D 06 3
Didcot to Banbury D 02 0
Didcot to Swindon C 84 2
Didcot to Winchester C 13 3
Dorset & Somerset Narrow Gauge D 76 4
Douglas to Peel C 88 5
Douglas to Port Erin C 55 9
Douglas to Ramsey D 39 X
Dovers Tramways B 24 3
Dover to Ramsgate A 78 9
E
Ealing to Slough C 42 7
Eastbourne to Hastings A 27 4 OOP
East Cornwall Mineral Railways D 22 5
East Croydon to Three Bridges A 53 3
East Grinstead - Branch Lines to A 07 X
East Ham & West Ham Tramways B 52 9
East Kent Light Railway A 61 4 OOP
East London - Branch Lines of C 44 3
East London Line B 80 4
East Ridings Secret Resistance D 21 7
Edgware & Willesden Tramways C 18 4
Effingham Junction - BLs around A 74 6
Eltham & Woolwich Tramways B 74 X OOP
Ely to Kings Lynn C 53 2
Ely to Norwich C 90 7
Embankment & Waterloo Tramways B 41 3
Enfield & Wood Green Trys C 03 6 OOP
Enfield Town & Palace Gates - BL to D 32 2
Epsom to Horsham A 30 4
Euston to Harrow & Wealdstone C 89 3
Exeter & Taunton Tramways B 32 4
Exeter to Barnstaple B 15 4
Exeter to Newton Abbot C 49 4
Exeter to Tavistock B 69 3
Exmouth - Branch Lines to B 00 6
F
Fairford - Branch Line to A 52 5
Falmouth, Helston & St. Ives - BL to C 74 5
Fareham to Salisbury A 67 3
Faversham to Dover B 05 7
Felixstowe & Aldeburgh - BL to D 20 9
Fenchurch Street to Barking C 20 6
Festiniog - 50 yrs of enterprise C 83 4
Festiniog in the Fifties B 68 5
Festiniog in the Sixties B 91 X
Finsbury Park to Alexandra Palace C 02 8
Frome to Bristol B 77 4
Fulwell - Trams, Trolleys & Buses D 11 X
G
Gloucester to Bristol D 35 7
Gloucester to Cardiff D 66 7
Gosport & Horndean Trys B 92 8
Gosport - Branch Lines around A 36 3
Great Yarmouth Tramways D 13 6
Greece Narrow Gauge D 72 1
Greenwich & Dartford Tramways B 14 6 OOP
Grimsby & Cleethorpes Trolleybuses D 86 1
Guildford to Redhill A 63 0 OOP
H
Hammersmith & Hounslow Trys C 33 8
Hampshire Narrow Gauge D 36 5
Hampshire Waterways A 84 3 OOP
Hampstead & Highgate Tramways B 53 7
Harrow to Watford D 14 4
Hastings to Ashford A 37 1
Hastings Tramways B 18 9
Hastings Trolleybuses B 81 2 OOP
Hawkhurst - Branch Line to A 66 5
Hay-on-Wye - Branch Lines around D92 6
Hayling - Branch Line to A 12 6
Haywards Heath to Seaford A 28 2
Henley, Windsor & Marlow - BL to C77 X
Hereford to Newport D 54 3
Hexham to CarlisleD 75 6
Hitchin to Peterborough D 07 1
Holborn & Finsbury Tramways B 79 0
Holborn Viaduct to Lewisham A 81 9
Horsham - Branch Lines to A 02 9
Huddersfield Trolleybuses C 92 3
Hull Tramways D60 8
Hull Trolleybuses D 24 1
Huntingdon - Branch Lines around A 93 2
I
Ilford & Barking Tramways B 61 8
Ilford to Shenfield C 97 4
Ilfracombe - Branch Line to B 21 9
Ilkeston & Glossop Tramways D 40 3
Industrial Rlys of the South East A 09 6
Ipswich to Saxmundham C 41 9
Ipswich Trolleybuses D 59 4
Isle of Wight Lines - 50 yrs C 12 5
K
Keighley Tramways & Trolleybuses D 83 7
Kent & East Sussex Waterways A 72 X
Kent Narrow Gauge C 45 1
Kent Seaways - Hoys to Hovercraft D 79 9
Kingsbridge - Branch Line to C 98 2
Kingston & Hounslow Loops A 83 5 OOP
Kingston & Wimbledon Tramways B 56 1
Kingswear - Branch Line to C 17 6
L
Lambourn - Branch Line to C 70 2
Launceston & Princetown - BL to C 19 2
Lewisham & Catford Tramways B 26 X OOP
Lewisham to Dartford A 92 4
Lines around Wimbledon B 75 8
Liverpool Street to Chingford D 01 2
Liverpool Street to Ilford C 34 6
Liverpool Tramways - Eastern C 04 4
Liverpool Tramways - Northern C 46 X
Liverpool Tramways - Southern C 23 0
London Bridge to Addiscombe B 20 0
London Bridge to East Croydon A 58 4
London Chatham & Dover Railway A 88 6
London Termini - Past and Proposed D 00 4
London to Portsmouth Waterways B 43 X
Longmoor - Branch Lines to A 41 X
Looe - Branch Line to C 22 2
Lyme Regis - Branch Line to A 45 2
Lynton - Branch Line to B 04 9
M
Maidstone & Chatham Tramways B 40 5
Maidstone Trolleybuses C 00 1 OOP
March - Branch Lines around B 09 X
Margate & Ramsgate Tramways C 52 4
Marylebone to Rickmansworth D49 7
Midhurst - Branch Lines around A 49 5
Midhurst - Branch Lines to A 01 0 OOP
Military Defence of West Sussex A 23 1
Military Signals, South Coast C 54 0
Minehead - Branch Line to A 80 0
Mitcham Junction Lines B 01 4
Mitchell & company C 59 1
Monmouthshire Eastern Valleys D 71 3
Moreton-in-Marsh to Worcester D 26 8
Moretonhampstead - BL to C 27 3
Mountain Ash to Neath D 80 2
N
Newbury to Westbury C 66 4
Newcastle to Hexham D 69 1
Newcastle Trolleybuses D 78 0
Newport (IOW) - Branch Lines to A 26 6
Newquay - Branch Lines to C 71 0
Newton Abbot to Plymouth C 60 5
Northern France Narrow Gauge C 75 3
North East German Narrow Gauge D 44 6
North Kent Tramways B 44 8
North London Line B 94 4
North Woolwich - BLs around C 65 6
Norwich Tramways C 40 0
Nottinghamshire & Derbyshire T/B D 63 2
Nottinghamshire & Derbyshire T/W D 53 5
O
Orpington to Tonbridge B 03 0 OOP
Oxford to Bletchley D57 8
Oxford to Moreton-in-Marsh D 15 2
P
Paddington to Ealing C 37 0
Paddington to Princes Risborough C 81 8
Padstow - Branch Line to B 54 5
Plymouth - BLs around B 98 7
Plymouth to St. Austell C 63 X
Pontypool to Mountain Ash D 65 9
Porthmadog 1954-94 - BL around B 31 6
Porthmadog to Blaenau B 50 2 OOP
Portmadoc 1923-46 - BL around B 13 8
Portsmouths Tramways B 72 3
Portsmouth to Southampton A 31 2
Portsmouth Trolleybuses C 73 7
Potters Bar to Cambridge D 70 5
Princes Risborough - Branch Lines to D 05 5
Princes Risborough to Banbury C 85 0
R
Railways to Victory C 16 8/7 OOP
Reading to Basingstoke B 27 8
Reading to Didcot C 79 6
Reading to Guildford A 47 9 OOP
Reading Tramways B 87 1
Reading Trolleybuses C 05 2
Redhill to Ashford A 73 8
Return to Blaenau 1970-82 C 64 8
Rickmansworth to Aylesbury D 61 6
Roman Roads of Hampshire D 67 5
Roman Roads of Surrey C 61 3
Roman Roads of Sussex C 48 6
Romneyrail C 32 X
Ryde to Ventnor A 19 3
S
Salisbury to Westbury B 39 1
Salisbury to Yeovil B 06 5 OOP
Saxmundham to Yarmouth C 69 9
Saxony Narrow Gauge D 47 0
Seaton & Eastbourne Tramways B 76 6 OOP
Seaton & Sidmouth - Branch Lines to A 95 9
Secret Sussex Resistance B 82 0
SECR Centenary album C 11 7
Selsey - Branch Line to A 04 5
Sheerness - Branch Lines around B 16 2
Shepherds Bush to Uxbridge T/Ws C 28 1
Shrewsbury - Branch Line to A 86 X
Sierra Leone Narrow Gauge D 28 4
Sittingbourne to Ramsgate A 90 8
Slough to Newbury C 56 7
Solent - Creeks, Crafts & Cargoes D 52 7
Southamptons Tramways B 33 2
Southampton to Bournemouth A 42 8
Southend-on-Sea Tramways B 28 6
Southern France Narrow Gauge C 47 8
Southwark & Deptford Tramways B 38 3
Southwold - Branch Line to A 15 0
South Eastern & Chatham Railways C 08
South London Line B 46 4
South London Tramways 1903-33 D 10 1
South London Tramways 1933-52 D 89 6
St. Albans to Bedford D 08 X
St. Austell to Penzance C 67 2
St. Pancras to Barking D 68 3
St. Pancras to St. Albans C 78 8
Stamford Hill Tramways B 85 5
Steaming through Cornwall B 30 8 OOP
Steaming through Kent A 13 4 OOP
Steaming through the Isle of Wight A 56 8
Steaming through West Hants A 69 X
Stratford upon avon to Birmingham D 77
Stratford upon Avon to Cheltenham C 25
Strood to Paddock Wood B 12 X OOP
Surrey Home Guard C 57 5
Surrey Narrow Gauge C 87 7
Surrey Waterways A 51 7 OOP
Sussex Home Guard C 24 9
Sussex Narrow Gauge C 68 0
Sussex Shipping Sail, Steam & Motor D 2
Swanley to Ashford B 45 6
Swindon to Bristol C 96 6
Swindon to Gloucester D46 2
Swindon to Newport D 30 6
Swiss Narrow Gauge C 94 X
T
Talyllyn - 50 years C 39 7
Taunton to Barnstaple B 60 X
Taunton to Exeter C 82 6
Tavistock to Plymouth B 88 X
Tees-side Trolleybuses D 58 6
Tenterden - Branch Line to A 21 5
Thanet's Tramways B 11 1 OOP
Three Bridges to Brighton A 35 5
Tilbury Loop C 86 9
Tiverton - Branch Lines around C 62 1
Tivetshall to Beccles D 41 1
Tonbridge to Hastings A 44 4
Torrington - Branch Lines to B 37 5
Tunbridge Wells - Branch Lines to A 32 0
Twickenham & Kingston Trys C 35 4
Two-Foot Gauge Survivors C 21 4 OOP
U
Upwell - Branch Line to B 64 2
V
Victoria & Lambeth Tramways B 49 9
Victoria to Bromley South A 98 3
Victoria to East Croydon A 40 1 OOP
Vivarais C 31 1 OOP
W
Walthamstow & Leyton Tramways B 65 0
Waltham Cross & Edmonton Trys C 07 9
Wandsworth & Battersea Tramways B 63
Wantage - Branch Line to D 25 X
Wareham to Swanage - 50 yrs D 09 8
War on the Line A 10 X
War on the Line VIDEO + 88 0
Waterloo to Windsor A 54 1
Waterloo to Woking A 38 X
Watford to Leighton Buzzard D 45 4
Wenford Bridge to Fowey C 09 5
Westbury to Bath B 55 3
Westbury to Taunton C 76 1
West Cornwall Mineral Railways D 48 9
West Croydon to Epsom B 08 1
West German Narrow Gauge D93 4
West London - Branch Lines of C 50 8
West London Line B 84 7
West Sussex Waterways A 24 X OOP
West Wiltshire - Branch Lines of D 12 8
Weymouth - Branch Lines around A 65 7
Willesden Junction to Richmond B 71 5
Wimbledon to Beckenham C 58 3
Wimbledon to Epsom B 62 6
Wimborne - Branch Lines around A 97 5
Wisbech - Branch Lines around C 01 X
Wisbech 1800-1901 C 93 1
Woking to Alton A 59 2
Woking to Portsmouth A 25 8
Woking to Southampton A 55 X
Wolverhampton Trolleybuses D 85 3
Woolwich & Dartford Trolleys B 66 9
Worcester to Hereford D 38 1
Worthing to Chichester A 06 1
Y
Yeovil - 50 yrs change C 38 9
Yeovil to Dorchester A 76 2 OOP
Yeovil to Exeter A 91 6
York Tramways & Trolleybuses D 82 9